The Mexican Cult of Death in Myth, Art and Literature

The Mexican Cult of Death in Myth, Art and Literature

BARBARA BRODMAN, PH.D.

iUniverse, Inc.
Bloomington

The Mexican Cult of Death in Myth, Art and Literature

iUniverse books may be ordered through booksellers or by contacting:

iUniverse
1663 Liberty Drive
Bloomington, IN 47403
www. iuniverse. com
1-800-Authors (1-800-288-4677)

ISBN: 978-1-4620-2261-8 (sc)
ISBN: 978-1-4620-2262-5 (ebk)

Library of Congress Control Number: 2011908295

Printed in the United States of America

iUniverse rev. date: 06/08/2011

Also by Barbara Brodman

The Mexican Cult of Death in Myth and Literature

Looking For Mr. Guevara: A Journey Through South America

The Global Warming Answer Book

For Elenore and Wayland Campbell

Table of Contents

Preface

The first edition of this book was released in 1976. Since then, much has changed in Mexico. Even before the passage of the North American Free Trade Agreement in 1994, the influence of Western—particularly U. S. —popular culture, entrance into the Age of Information, and the urbanization of the Mexican population had contributed to a changed worldview for many Mexicans. I had expected that this change might obscure or eliminate the Mexican cult of death as a dominant expression of worldview and culture, particularly in urban areas. It appears that I was mistaken.

In major cities of Mexico, particularly among members of the underground economy, devotees of *la Santa Muerte* continue to grow in both numbers and fervor.

In the Mexican countryside, where modernization is minimal, both the traditional worldview and the cult of death are alive and strong; though it is to be noted that, in Mexico, as elsewhere, traditionalism and poverty are far too closely linked. From this reality derives the fear that integration into the political and economic mainstream will significantly diminish salient aspects of the traditional worldview, chief among which is the Mexican cult of death.

The Zapatista rebels in the impoverished yet resource-rich south of Mexico, who recognize the threat of integration to traditional cultures and values, have, from the beginning, stressed the need to improve the quality of life of indigenous Mexicans without sacrificing key aspects of their culture.

That the cult of death remains a salient feature of the traditional worldview is reflected in the writings of EZLN Subcomandante Marcos and other Zapatista writers. To illustrate this point, I have added to the

1976 text a chapter entitled "From Sacrificial Fire to Fire in the Mind: The Mexican Cult of Death in Modern Literature and Politics."

In the 2011 edition, I have also added to the discussion of the cult of death in Mexican literature a chapter that presents a unique interpretation of the life and art of Frida Kahlo, whose works helped introduce the Mexican cult of death to the world.

Spanish citations used in the 1976 edition have been retained, though the reader may now find most of the works alluded to in English translation.

B. B.

Introduction

The word death is not pronounced in New York, in Paris, in London, because it burns the lips. The Mexican, in contrast, is familiar with death, jokes about it, caresses it, sleeps with it, celebrates it, it is one of his favorite toys and his most steadfast love. True, there is perhaps as much fear in his attitude as in that of others, but at least death is not hidden away: he looks at it face to face, with impatience, disdain or irony. . . .Our contempt for death is not at odds with the cult we have made of it.

The Labyrinth of Solitude

Thus Octavio Paz describes a cultural phenomenon that has for centuries fascinated scholars and aficionados of virtually every field of Mexican studies, "el culto a la muerte," the cult of death, a term that readily calls to the mind of anyone familiar with Mexico and her culture the unusually constant place of death in the minds and lives of the Mexican people. Death is, so to speak, a constant companion of the Mexican in his or her journey through life.

The purpose of this study is twofold. It is primarily to discuss the literary manifestations of the Mexican cult of death, a topic that, because of its vastness, I have chosen to limit primarily to the discussion of its occurrences in 20th century Mexican short fiction of the period 1947-60. Representative authors and works are Juan Rulfo, *El llano en llamas*; José Revueltas, *Dormir en tierra*; Rosario Castellanos, *Ciudad Real*; Carlos Fuentes, *Los días enmascarados,* Guadalupe Dueñas, *Tiene la noche un árbol*; and Eraclio Zepeda, *Benzulul.*

The fame of the first four of these authors rests heavily upon the novel, though I have chosen to discuss the manifestations of the cult of death in their short stories. My reasons for doing so are the following: First, I feel that the short story, dealing as it does génerolly with one theme or aspect of the world it depicts, is the ideal literary form in which to seek manifestations of an isolated phenomenon like the cult of death. Also, I feel that as a genre the short story has suffered unfair and frequent critical neglect, and I agree with José Lopez Valdizón when he says, "no hay genera literario fácil y el cuento está considerado entre los más difíciles. Esto por su extension, su dinámica y la síntesis que presuponen tales condiciones. . . .el cuento es esencia y obedece a una estructura propia e intransferible"[*Comunidad* 3(14):369]. Additionally, I have found that in regard to manifestations of the cult of death, little, if anything, would be gained by discussing them in relation to the novel rather than the short story, for manifestations of the cult of death in the novels of these authors, though slightly more embellished, are generally highly consistent with those found in their short stories.

A second purpose of this study is to discuss the historical bases of the phenomenon, for the cult of death in Mexico is not merely a literary phenomenon, nor is it a recent one. It is, rather, a social phenomenon whose roots are buried deep in the soil formed by the union of two distinct cultures, each of which possessed a perceptible cult of death and each of which imparted certain aspects of that cult to the culture of which it was co-creator. I therefore feel that a necessary preliminary to any discussion of the manifestations of this phenomenon in its contemporary state must be a discussion of the historical bases upon which it was founded, and since we are concerned primarily with the literary manifestations of the phenomenon, a discussion of its literary bases is also in order.

It should be noted, though, that the purpose of this book is not to study literary influences, but rather to establish the existence of a state of mind and to use as proof its sustained reiteration as a literary theme in pre-Conquest and contemporary literature. Literary references in the first three chapters of this study are therefore not to be interpreted as having directly influenced the later works discussed in Chapter Four. They are provided, rather, as an aid to acquiring a more concrete background for the understanding of the term "cult of death."

Before beginning the discussion of the manifestations of the cult of death in the 20th century Mexican short story, I shall therefore discuss the historical and literary bases of the phenomenon, relating them to the two pre-Conquest cultures from which modern Mexican culture derives; and I shall examine the sociological and psychological implications of the cult, showing it to constitute an integral part of the psyche of the Mexican, thereby logically manifesting itself in contemporary Mexican literature.

To provide additional dimension, the 2011 edition of this book expands the analysis of the Mexican cult of death beyond the realms of myth and literature to the areas of art and politics, incorporating discussions of Zapatista literature and politics and the life and art of Frida Kahlo.

In this manner I hope to provide a far more comprehensive and defined picture of the cult of death and its relationship to arts and letters in Mexico than has heretofore been provided by social scientists or literary scholars. One finds that the Mexican cult of death as a social phenomenon has been discussed and alluded to by scholars in numerous fields. Yet, no one has attempted to combine in one study the perspectives of a variety of disciplines to provide a succinct, comprehensive analysis of the origins and nature of the phenomenon and its relationship to contemporary literature and culture. This I propose to do.

The opposition between life and death was not so absolute to the ancient Mexicans as it is to us. Life extended into death, and vice versa. Death was not the natural end of life but one phase of an infinite cycle. Life, death and resurrection were stages of a cosmic process which repeated itself continuously. Life had no higher function than to flow into death, its opposite and complement; and death, in turn, was not an end in itself; man fed the insatiable hunger of life with his death.

Octavio Paz

A Ayocuan

Entretéjanse flores azules y flores color de fuego:
tu corazón y tu palabra, oh príncipe chichimeca Ayocuan.
Por un breve instante hazlas tuyas aquí en la tierra.

Lloro porque nuestra muerte las destruye,
ay, destruya nuestras obras: los bellos cantares,
por un breve instante házlos tuyos en la tierra.

Anonymous

1

Historical and Literary Bases of the Cult of Death in Mexico

To understand the bases of the Mexican cult of death, one must look back first to the basic religious beliefs of pre-Conquest Mexico, for every phase of life throughout the development of Mexican culture was integrally bound with religion. According to that religion, the world in which the pre-Conquest Mexican lived was the fifth world, or Sun, to have been created, the other four having been destroyed one by one before the fifth world came into being. That world was to meet the same fate as its predecessors, the means of destruction this time, as determined by the birth sign *naui ollin*, being a series of cataclysms culminating in the release of "monsters of the twilight who await the fatal hour beneath the western sky, [and] will swarm out and hurl themselves upon the last survivors" [1:96].

It was a world that had been created through the blood and sacrifice of the gods. The story of that creation, as it was told by native informers to Fray Bernardino de Sahagún shortly after the Conquest, is as follows:

> 4. -Decían que antes que hubiese día en el mundo que se juntaron los dioses en aquel lugar que se llama *Teotihuacan*, . . . dijeron los unos a los otros dioses: "¿Quien tendra cargo de alumbrar al mundo?"

5. -Luego a estas palabras respondió un dios que se llamaba *Tecuciztécatl*, y dijo: "Yo tomo cargo de alumbrar al mundo." Luego otra vez hablaron los dioses, y dijeron: "¿Quién sera otro?"

7. -Uno de los lios [sic] de que no se hacía cuenta y era buboso, no hablaba sino oía lo que los otros dioses decían, y los otros habláronle y dijéronle: "Sé tú el que alumbres, bubosito." Y él de buena voluntad obedeció a lo que Ie mandaron y respondió: "En merced recibo lo que me habéis mandado, sea así."

12. -Después que se acabaron las cuatro noches de su penitencia, . . .

13. - . . .ardió el fuego cuatro días.

14. - . . .y luego los dos sobredichos se pusieron delante del fuego, . . .

16. -[TecuciztécatI] cuatro veces probó, pero nunca se osó echar. . . .

17. - . . .los dioses luego hablaron a *Nanautzin* y dijeron: "!Ea pues, Nanauatzin, prueba tú!"

18. - Y como Ie hubieron hablado los dioses, esforzóse y cerrando los ojos arremetió y echóse en el fuego, . . .y como vió TecuciztécatI que se había echado en el fuego, y ardía, arremetió y echóse en el fuego.

21. -Después que ambos se hubieron arrojado en el fuego, y después que se hubieron quemado. . . .

23. - . . . los dioses se hincaron de rodillas para esperar a dónde saldría Nanauatzin hecho sol. . . .

25. - . . .primero salió el sol y tras él salió la luna; por el orden que entraron en el fuego por el mismo salieron hechos sol y luna.

26. - . . .tenían igual luz con que alumbraban. . . .

27. - . . .Y luego uno de los dioses fué corriendo y dió con un conejo en la cara a TecuciztécatI, y oscurecióle la cara y ofuscóle el resplandor, y quedó como ahora está su cara.

28. -Después que hubieron salido ambos sobre la tierra estuvieron quedos, sin moverse de un lugar el sol y la luna; y los dioses otra vez se hablaron, y dijeron: "¿Cómo podemos vivir? ¿No se menea el sol? ¿Hemos de vivir entre los villanos? Muramos todos y hagámosle que resucite por nuestra muerte."

29. -Y luego el Aire se encargó de matar a todos los dioses y matólos . . .

31. - . . .y después que el sol comenzó a caminar la luna se estuvo queda en el lugar donde estaba.

32. - . . .de esta manera se desviaron el uno del otro y así salen en
    diversos tiempos . . .
[2:1,258-61]

In this theory of creation through sacrifice lay the latent seed from
which would spring, years later, the bloody religious ritual of the Aztecs[1],
based on the rationalization that "if only the death of the gods could
make possible the movement and life of the Sun, then only the sacrifice
of men, who play the role of the gods on earth, can maintain its life and
motion" [3:31]. Only through self-sacrifice could man postpone the
cataclysms that were destined to put an end to the Sun and preserve it
from the same destiny of its predecessors.

Thus, the earth was born of death and doomed to catastrophe.
And the Mexican, by his very concept of creation, was deprived of
any control over his life or destiny. His was a fatalistic concept of life,
every phase of which was ruled by determinism and overshadowed by
the omnipresent specter of death. Thus, in his book on Mexican art,
Justino Fernández speaks of the first Mexican temples as "proof of an
ancient but already well-developed culture, with evidence of a cult of
the dead" and points out that "the image of death appears in Mexican
art in one way or another from the earliest period to the present time"
[4:9,13]. In the words of Jacques Soustelle, "Death and life are no more

---

1   A brief explanation of terms may be in order at this time. The term
    "Aztec" refers to the language and people of Tenochtítlan. It is the
    term adopted by the Spaniards based upon the mythological place from
    which the Aztecs believed they came, Lake Aztlán. Most students of
    language refer to the immediate group of Uto-Aztecan languages, of
    which Aztec was one, as Nahuatl. Classical Nahuatl is a "dead" literary
    language based upon the language of Tenochtítlan and reduced to
    writing shortly after the Conquest by the Franciscan missionaries. It is
    from this language that the works cited herein have been translated. I
    use the term "Nahuatl" to refer not only to the language, but also to
    the peoples and cultures who used this language prior to the Conquest,
    exclusive, that is, of the Aztecs, to whom I refer as such. I have also
    used the more general term "Mexican" interchangeably with all of the
    above. This I find is a tendency common among modern Mexicans.

than two sides of the same reality; from the earliest times the potters of Tlatilco made a double face, one half alive and the other skull-like, and the dualism is also to be found in innumerable documents. Perhaps, no people in history have been so much haunted by the grim presence of death as the Mexicans, but for them life came out of death as the young plant comes from the mouldering seed of the earth" [1:106].

As time went on these basic myths were embellished and expanded upon to form various religious sects. The most important of these prior to the appearance of the Aztecs as an organized tribe (ca. A. D. 1200) was that based upon the person and doctrine of Quetzalcóatl. This god-king was the inspiration for one of the world's truly beautiful religious myths, and his doctrine added a new dimension to Mexican religious philosophy and to the cult of death.

Quetzalcóatl appears to have been ruler, for approximately twenty years, of the Toltec city of Tula, built between A. D. 900-1156. He was conceived when his mother swallowed a stone of jade, a symbolic representation of the soul of man, suggesting his heavenly, spiritual origin. As a ruler he postulated a doctrine based upon prayer and penitence. Despite some wizards and sorcerers who encouraged him to accept human sacrifice, Quetzalcóatl was opposed to such practices, preaching instead the sacrifice of snakes and butterflies. High dignitaries, according to his doctrine, should be "virtuous, humble and peace-loving, considerate and prudent, not frivolous, but grave and austere and jealous of custom, loving, merciful, compassionate and a friend to all, and devout and fearful of god . . ." [5:27]. Knighthood was achieved through contemplation, humiliation, and detachment, the ceremony consisting of forty to seventy days of fasting and contemplation in a locked temple, subjection to taunts, insults, physical attacks, and filthy conditions, culminating in a visit to the Great Temple where the initiates received the doctrine by which they would live their lives. "The central part of these Tests of Initiation is the detachment taught by Quetzalcóatl as a means of liberation from duality" [5:68]; that is, the liberation of the spirit from the body, an obvious exaltation of the spiritual life. "It is significant that the demons who decide, because of Quetzalcóatl's irritating purity, to cause his downfall invent exactly the trick of 'giving him his body' . . . [5:56].

This the wizard Tezcatlipoca does first by showing to Quetzalcóatl his reflection in a mirror, then by tricking him into getting drunk and sleeping with a woman thereby breaking his vow of celibacy. Having committed these grave errors, Quetzalcóatl decides to leave his people and travel east to the shores of the "divine water," the gulf coast. There he sets himself on fire and burns to death. He descends into the region of the dead where he gathers up the bones of a dead man and woman and brings them to life with his own blood. On the eighth day he rises to the heavens to become the great star Venus, called by the Mexicans, "Quetzalcóatl." "The spiritual content of the Quetzalcóatl myth is self-evident. The anguish for his sin, his burning need for purification, and, also, the fire that converts him into light reveal a religious doctrine closely related to those humanity has known elsewhere under various symbolic languages" [5:54].

The blood of Quetzalcóatl, the "divine fire," symbolizes the blood of the Redeemer who, through his own sacrifice, brings about man's birth into spirituality. The soul follows the same symbolic route taken by Quetzalcóatl. "She descends from her celestial home and enters the darkness of matter only to rise again, glorious, at the moment of the body's dissolution. The myth of Quetzalcóatl signifies just this. The King's absolute purity refers to the state of the planet when it is still nothing but light. His sins and remorse correspond to the phenomenon of the incarnation of this light and the painful, but necessary, assumption of human form; his abandonment of the things of this world and the fatal fire he builds with his own hands show the precepts which have to be followed if human existence is not to be lost, the attainment of eternal unity through detachment from and sacrifice of the transitory self" [5:59]. Thus, with Quetzalcóatl the concepts of death and sacrifice suffer no loss of importance as basic religious concepts, but take on a more symbolic significance.

We see, then, that death and sacrifice were outstanding elements of the religious myths of the Mexican peoples, indicating that from the beginning death was accorded a position of extreme importance in their culture. Everything had been created through the death of the gods, and with destruction it was wholly bound. With Quetzalcóatl and the religious doctrine that grew up around him, the profoundly deterministic nature of Mexican religious philosophy was tempered to allow for the possibility of man's being able to achieve some sort of spiritual state which would allow him to detach himself from his finite world. It was with this particular doctrine that the Mexicans came closest to exhibiting any real kinship to the religious doctrine of their future conquerors. But long before any contact between these cultures could take place, the doctrine of Quetzalcóatl had been corrupted and replaced by a new doctrine.

With the Aztecs and the advent of the Era of Huitzilopochtli. the doctrine of Quetzalcóatl lost much of its symbolic significance. "The idea of feeding the sun with a symbolic heart, created within man's psyche, was very soon distorted. Offerings to the gods made in flowers picked from the meadows and cornfields became offerings of enemy hearts torn out" [5:75]. "The laws of interior preparation revealed by Quetzalcóatl were used by the Aztecs to prop up their bloody state. The mystic union with the divinity, which the individual could achieve only by successive steps and after a life of contemplation and penitence, was thenceforth considered to be the result merely of the manner of a man's death. We are here dealing with low witchcraft, the material transmission of human energy to the sun" [5:28].

A thorough discussion of the reasons behind the Aztecs' development of their bloody, death-oriented religious rites would be far too long and superfluous to the main topic of this study to be attempted here, but it is worthwhile to note that the *guerras floridas*, waged with the primary purpose of acquiring sacrificial victims, and the sacrificial rites themselves, were by no means purely religious manifestations, but also extremely powerful and effective political tools. Thus, a death cult such as we see in Mexico today is but a logical outgrowth of a culture that was once one of the most death-oriented in the world.

Much of Aztec thought may be attributed to the teachings of the powerfully influential priest-politician Tlacaélel. It was he who persuaded the Aztecs that their god was Huitzilopochtli, the Sun, and that by providing him with enough of the vital energy contained in the blood and hearts of their own kind, they could postpone indefinitely the destruction of the fifth Sun. Therefore, instead of a religion oriented more toward spiritual concerns based on an absolute assurance of the world's impending physical destruction, a religion sprang up in which the primary concern was for the maintenance of the physical state of the world, devoid of any concern for the individual.

> According to Aztec religion. . . .man has no other aim on
> earth but to feed the Sun with his own blood, without which
> the Sun will die of exhaustion. This tragic dilemma obliges
> him to choose between indulging in massacre or bringing
> about the end of the world. So each victim, aware of his
> cosmic mission, cheerfully allowed his heart to be torn out,
> and . . .the Aztec chroniclers preserved the names of certain
> warriors whose specially heroic deaths were held up for
> emulation. But, if we do not passively accept these official
> declarations, if we refuse to regard it as natural that customs
> should be perpetuated which, whatever their time and place,
> are monstrous, we may begin to perceive that we are here
> dealing with a totalitarian state of which the philosophy
> included an utter contempt for the individual. . . . According
> to the testimony of all the chroniclers, Spanish and native
> alike, it appears on the surface that any freedom of thought
> or action was inconceivable in the Aztec world.   [5:14]

Certainly many sacrificial victims willingly, with great pride, mounted the temple steps to have their hearts torn out, considering themselves saviors of the world and reincarnations of the gods who had performed a similar act to create life. Also, since the Aztecs believed that it was the manner of a man's death and not his conduct in life that determined his spiritual destiny, death in battle or on the sacrificial stone was often pursued as it carried with it the reward of attaining one of the most desirable of the several Aztec heavens.

The stories of ritual sacrifices in which the victim went with willingness to meet his fate are many in both native and Spanish chronicles. They reflect the extent to which the bloody doctrine of the Aztecs had permeated the minds and everyday lives of the people who lived under its sway.

Every month, and there were eighteen in the Aztec solar calendar, had its ceremonies and festivals with the usual sacrifices. Sometimes sacrificial victims were destined by birth to represent a particular god on the sacrificial stone; sometimes the victims were prisoners of war; sometimes they were women, and, sometimes, children. Most were laid across the convex sacrificial stone, arms and legs held down by four priests while the fifth slashed the breast with an obsidian knife, pulled out the still-beating heart, and burnt it as an offering to the god. The body was then rolled down the temple steps where it was prepared by other priests for a cannibalistic communion rite, often partaken of by the entire population.

Other sacrificial rites were those to the fire god. Huehueteotl, in which victims were first thrown into a fire and then fished out still alive to have their living hearts torn out and offered to the god, or those in the last month of the year, in which victims were tied to a stake and killed with arrows. It was also permissible and common practice for wealthy merchants and dignitaries to buy slaves in the market place to be used as sacrificial victims and served to guests in their homes. In some months there were weeks of ceremonies and parades in which the priests danced in the flayed skins of sacrificial victims. Anyone of these spectacles, to us so abominable, was a common and accepted occurrence to the pre-Conquest Mexican.

This may help to explain how, in the fifth month of every year, a young prisoner of war, fattened and treated as a god for one year, went proudly and stoically to his death, sincerely believing himself to be the incarnation of the god Tezcatlipoca; or how a famous captured Tlaxcallan general, Tlalhuicoltzin, having refused the freedom and honors offered to him by Moctezuma II by virtue of his gallant past record, should accept the command of Moctezuma's armies in a war against the Tarascans, defeat them completely, return loaded with booty and prisoners, and still refuse his freedom, begging for and receiving instead "the honorable death of a soldier on the sacrificial stone of Him who had vanquished him, the 'teotl' Huitzilopochtli" [7:117].

These are only a very few of the many examples of Mexicans who had been indoctrinated sufficiently in their bloody religion to be able to accept and support the ritual of human sacrifice, even when the sacrifice was their own. But it is evident that many looked upon these rites with fear and horror and saw them as mere tools of political oppression. The *guerras floridas*, waged in theory for the purely religious purpose of securing sacrificial victims, were in reality "concebidas con un interés político. . . .Si se piensa que durante los cuarenta años de su formación el Estado azteca ha vivido sobre la ley de la fuerza, nos persuadimos que la santificación de la violencia era la única salida lógica nada más eficaz para dominar una población, en gran parte constituida por hordas mercenarias y por sobrevivientes de ciudades devastadas, que el terror sagrado que se instala entonces sobre la metrópoli" [8:147].

"'We do not believe,' said the Aztecs, 'we fear'" [9:116]. And how else could one explain the existence of written rules concerning procedures in the event of unwillingness to be sacrificed or penalties—of death, of course—to be imposed upon anyone refusing to witness a sacrifice? Or, why else would cities such as Tlaxcala and Texcoco, with the same religious tradition as the Aztecs, so readily ally themselves with the Spaniards against Moctezuma? "This hostility towards the Aztecs seems to show that the belief in a holy war which the latter so freely propagated has been taken more seriously by modern students than by the Mesoamerican peoples themselves. If faith in the general cosmic need for ritual killing had existed, these betrayals would have been unthinkable, the more so since, as archaeology has proven, the Nahuatl religion was firmly rooted throughout Mexico" [5:44].

It appears, then, that Aztec religion was a corruption of traditional Nahuatl religion and that it was almost entirely the result of political necessity. But whether the people feared or believed in this religion, the fact still remains that such an extremely death-oriented religion did exist and that it created the situation whereby, regardless of whether they feared it or believed in it, death was a constant in the life of every Mexican during the Aztec era.

It is most difficult for the European or North American to truly understand the Mexican concept of death and its relationship to life. We, who are so extraordinarily afraid of death, though we have created numerous interpretations of the phenomenon, have always seen it as something opposed to life, in contradistinction to it. The Mexican, on the other hand, from his most primitive myth of creation, saw life as indivisibly united to death. Together these two states of being created the whole of the natural order of things. One without the other would have been incomplete and inconceivable; and, therefore, one was not preferable to the other. This explains the frequent representation of the dual aspect of life in Mexican art—the living aspect of one side of a sculpture and the skeletal aspect of the other—and the realistic representations of death so often reflected there.

Since an awareness of death permeated every aspect of the life of the ancient Mexican, it is understandable that it provided the motive for some of his finest art. In literature, death was an outstanding motif.

Since "to die . . .was to accomplish an act of incalculably far-reaching potentialities" [9:115], it was quite logically a major preoccupation of the great ancient Nahuatl poet-philosophers. Let us examine, then, some representative examples of pre-Conquest Nahuatl literature and see how they reflect the authors' artistic preoccupation with death.

I have chosen to restrict the discussion of pre-Conquest Nahuatl literature to the field of lyric poetry. This I do not only for the sake of brevity, but also because I feel that lyric poetry was the best vehicle for personal expression in pre-Conquest Mexico, and it is with the establishment of the existence of a cult of death in the minds of the people of the culture, and its subsequent manifestation in their literature, that I am most concerned. That death was an outstanding theme in other forms of poetry, epic and dramatic, and in the prose of the period also is certain, but these genres, being vehicles more of religious and political expression, represent what might be called the causal rather than the effectual genres of pre-Conquest Nahuatl literature as they relate to the cult of death.

Angel María Garibay, one of the world's foremost authorities on ancient Nahuatl literature, divides lyric poetry into five categories. The first of these contains essentially three types of lyric poems, Cuauhcuicatl, Teuccuicatl, and Yaocuicatl (*canto de águilas, canto de príncipes,* and *canto de guerra*), which celebrate "la santidad de la guerra, la dicha de los que en ella mueren, la memoria de los grandes caudillos" [10:1,85]. As is to be expected, death is a predominant theme in these poems, death in battle or as a prisoner of war on the sacrificial stone is presented as being superior to any other form of death and, therefore, is to be actively pursued, for the soldier killed in battle and the sacrificial victim attained the highest of Aztec heavens, becoming companions of the Sun. Thus, the Aztec warrior-poet cries out,

> ¡Corazón mío, no temas:
> en medio a la llanura quiere mi corazón
> la muerte de obsidiana:
> solo quiere mi corazon
> la muerte en guerra!   [10:1,217]

> For he who dies the death of a warrior
> goes before, goes to be with,
> in order to stay with the sun.   [11:107]

The Xochicuicatl, or *canto de flores*, is comparable to Western idyllic poetry, though having as its own peculiar characteristic "la tendencia a la reflexión, y la sombra de la muerte [que] baja leve y sutil sobre sus florecientes alegrías" [10:1,87]. The Mexican's natural tendency toward melancholy led him to envision beside each blooming flower one that was withered and faded. "Hay una melancolía que domina aún entre las canciones que monotonamente aluden a las flores. La flor puede ser un símbolo de esta poesía: efímera, fugaz, bella, perfumada, y, bien pronto, mudada en amarillos pétalos y en basura que arrebata el viento. Tal es la concepción de la vida y de la belleza en estos balbucientes poetas" [10:1, 189].

Thus, in the following poem, behind the exquisite imagery of strings of flowers flowing from the mouth of the poet, lies the omnipresent lesson of the ephemeral nature of man, who, like the flowers of spring, lasts but a moment and is gone.

> Comienzo a cantar, soy cantor:
> Repártanse flores, con ellas haya placer,
> con ellas haya felicidad en la tierra.
>
> Son tu riqueza, oh cantor:
> ¡Feliz tú que has merecido las flores,
> feliz tú que has merecido ver el canto!
> Tú distribuyes a los hombres aquí
> hilos de flores que salen de tu boca,
> tú para ellos las has tomado:
> Con ellas haya placer, con ellas haya felicidad en la
> tierra.
> Yo soy Yohyontzin: con avidez deseo las flores,
> me vivo cantando cantos floridos.
> Quiero y anhelo la amistad, la compañía, la unión:
> con avidez deseo las flores,
> me vivo cantando cantos floridos.
>
> Vengo a llorar, vengo a ponerme triste,
> Soy cantor y, ¿he de llevar mis flores?
> ¡Con ellas me ataviara yo en el Reino de la Sombra!

> Vengo a ponerme triste:
> ¡Sólo cual flor es reputado el hombre en la tierra;
> sólo por breve instante tenemos prestados flores de
> primavera!
> Gozad vosotros: yo me pongo triste.   [10:I,88]

Also in the *canto de flores* is expressed the idea of poetry, "flower and song," as a means of achieving immortality, "el guerrero daba flores de corazones; el que no era para guerra . . . daba cantos. Uno y otro perpetuaban su nombre en la tierra" [10:I,177].

> We will be gone to His house.
> but our word
> shall live here on earth.
> We will go. leaving behind
> our grief. our song.
> For this will be known.
> the song shall remain real.
> We will have gone to His house,
> but our word shall live here on earth.   [3:79]

Finally, the following poem offers a philosophy shared by most poets of this genre, that life is brief and that one should neither become too attached to it nor despise it for that reason. Instead, one should be like the butterfly flitting through life, enjoying its beauty and becoming a part of it.

> ¿Qué es lo que meditas? ¿Qué es lo que recuerdas,
> oh. amigo mío? ¿No gozas en tomar cantos?
> ¿No tienes el deseo de las flores del dador de vida?
> Goza junto a los tambores.
> aléjate cuando Ie plazca a tu corazón.

> La mariposa floreciente pasa entre los hombres:
> chupe la miel de nuestras flores.
> Con nuestros ramilletes, con nuestros abanicos,
> con el humo de nuestros cañutos se entrelaza
> y persiste en deleite junto a los tambores.   [10:I. 188]

Sadness and melancholy, then, pass like a fleeting shadow through the *canto de flores*. In the Icnocuicatl. the *canto de desolación, de orfandad*, they constitute the fundamental and almost sole themes. In this they are similar to the Western elegy, the *canto lírico*, in Spain.

Bitterness and desolation over the uncertainty of what lies ahead are clearly reflected in the following representative poems:

> I, Cuauhtencoztle. here I am suffering,
> What is, perchance true?
> Will my song still be real tomorrow?
> Are men perhaps real?
> What is it that will survive?
> Here we live, here we stay,
> but we are destitute, o my friends!   [3:82]

> ¿Sólo me iré semejante a las flores que fueron pereciendo?
>
> ¿Nada mi gloria será alguna vez?
> ¿Nada mi fama será en la tierra?
>
> ¡Siquiera flores, siquiera cantos!
> ¿Ay, qué hará mi corazón?
> ¡En vano venimos a pasar por la tierra!   [10:I,90-91]

In each of these poems, as in the *canto de desolación* in general, the inanity of life and the obsession with death are constant themes.

Another theme common to this type of poetry is the life-is-a-dream aspect, so ingeniously brought to life by Calderón in Spain and, here, combined with the popular comparison of man to a flower.

> "Sólo vinimos a dormir,
> sólo vinimos a soñar:
> ¡no es verdad, no es verdad que vinimos a vivir en la
> tierra:
> Cual cada primavera de la hierba así es nuestra hechura:
> viene y brota, viene y abre corolas nuestro corazón:
> algunas flores echa nuestro cuerpo: se marchita!"   [10:I,191]

In the following poem we pass from the universal themes reflected above to a topic unique to Nahuatl poetry.

> ¡Sólo te busco a ti, padre nuestro dador de la vida:
> sufriendo estoy: seas tú nuestro amigo,
> hablemos uno a otro tus hermosas palabras,
> digamos por que estoy triste:
> busco el deleite de tus flores,
> la alegrIa de tus cantos, tu riqueza!
>
> Dicen que en buen lugar, dentro del cielo,
> hay vida general, hay alegría:
> enhiestos están los atabales:
> es perpetuo el canto con el que se disipa
> nuestro llanto y nuestra tristeza:
>
> ¡es donde ellos viven, es su casa:
> ojalá lo supierais así, oh príncipes!   [10:I,192]

Here man is placed in all of his misery, before instinctively perceived, insuperable powers which leave him with a terror of his nothingness and a complex feeling of abandonment and fear, resignation and surrender, mixed all the while with a certain feeling of distrust.

The fourth category into which Garibay divides Nahuatl lyric poetry is that of religious poetry. As should be expected, given the religious background material presented earlier in the discussion of the historical bases of the death cult, death is a salient theme in this type of poetry. Constant reference is made to sacred war, sacrificial ritual, and the death of the gods and men. Thus, in the following segment from a longer religious poem, an abundant harvest is attributed to the abundant offering of sacrificial victims.

> ¡El humo de la hoguera! Hacen estruendo los escudos!
> ¡El dios de los cascabeles!
> Allí son tremoladas tus flores, oh Enemigo,
> hacen allí el estruendo las Aguilas, los Tigres.
>
> Tú te has mostrado amigo, gracia hiciste a los hombres:

hay ondular de llamas, el polvo amarillece:
van a brotar rajas flores, se esparcen, abren su corola.

En el agua floreciente de la hoguera
está la casa de las mariposas del escudo:
allí con dardos lee, extiende la pintura
en libros de divinas flores Motecuzoma en México.
¡Sustituyó nuestro alimento con sacrificados!

Oh dios Aguila, en tu mansión imperas:
allí con dardos lee, extiende la pintura
en libros de divinas flores Motecuzoma en Mexico.

¡Sustituyó nuestro alimento con sacrificados!   [10:I,136]

And in the following hymn sung before the ceremony of cremation, one sees the praise of death typical of this type of poetry.

"Awaken, already the sky is tinged with red,
already the dawn has come,
already the flame-colored pheasants are singing,
the fire-colored swallows,
already butterflies are on the wing."

For this reason the ancient ones said,
he who has died, he becomes a god.
They said: "He became a god there,"
which means that he died.   [3:62]

As is to be expected, given the important role that religion played in every aspect of the lives of the ancient Mexicans, this particular category of Nahuatl poetry often overlaps each of the other four categories proposed by Garibay and extends also into the realm of narrative poetry.

The last category is that of the *poema corto*, the character of which is defined by its size rather than by its content; for, judged by its content, it may fit into any one of the preceding categories. In their succinctness and intimate lyricality, these poems not only bespeak the

intellectual preoccupation of their authors with the theme of death, but also manifest a skill which renders them capable of competing with the best of the world's lyric poetry. Let us look at a few examples of these *pequeñas joyas de poesía lírica,* noting, as a characteristic of each, the author's persistent preoccupation with the theme of death.

Vida de Ilusión

¿Acaso es verdad que se vive en la tierra?
¿Acaso para siempre es la tierra?
¡Sólo un breve instante aquí!

Hasta las piedras finas se resquebrajan,
hasta el oro se destroza, hasta las plumas preciosas se desgarran,
¿Acaso para siempre es la tierra? ¡Sólo un breve instante! [12:31]

¡Animo!

¡No te amedrentes, corazón mío!
allá en el campo de batalla
ansío morir a filo de obsidiana.

Oh, los que estáis en la lucha:
yo ansío morir a filo de obsidiana.
Sólo quieren nuestros corazones la muerte gloriosa. [12:31]

Will I end as the flowers end?
Will glory avail me nothing
My passing through this world,
Shall it be dust?
Let me then be flowers
Or at least be many songs . . .
What sayest thou, o heart?
We pass this way, we do,
All in vain. [13:34]

In each of these categories of lyric poetry, death, and what lies beyond it is the outstanding preoccupation.

The schools of thought concerning death reflected in Nahuatl poetry appear to be essentially three in number. The first indicates an Epicurean/*Carpe diem* trend—that there is no afterlife; therefore, enjoy life on earth while you have it.

> Lloro y me aflijo cuando recuerdo
> que dejaremos las bellas flores, los bellos cantos.
> ¡Gocemos, cantemos, todos nos vamos . . .   [12:36]

> We do not come upon this earth a second time,
> O Chichimecan Princes! Let us enjoy life.   [13:33]

The second school of thought displays the definite influence of traditional religious belief in life after death, but also displays a great deal of doubt and uncertainty, as Quenamican, the very name of the place of the dead, implies,"the place where those, in one way or another, live. "Looking fearfully upon man's ultimate destiny, the poets of this school adopt a skeptical and questioning attitude.

> Perchance, are we really true beyond?
> Will we live where there is only sadness?
> Is it true, perchance is it not true? . . .
> How many can truthfully say
> that truth is or is not there?
> Let our hearts not be troubled.   [14:132]

The followers of the third school display a more positive attitude, believing in the positive power of flower and song and in the existence of a place beyond life where one might find happiness. Thus, in the following poem is displayed a confidence, not reflected in the poetry of the other two schools, that man may lift himself up and escape the ephemerality of a dreamlike world.

> Truly. earth is not the place of reality.
> Indeed, one must go elsewhere;
> beyond, happiness exists.

Or is it that we come to earth in vain?
Certainly some other place is the abode of life . . . .

Beyond is the place where one lives.
I would be lying to myself were I to say,
"Perhaps everything ends on this earth;
here do our lives end."

No, o Lord of the Close Vicinity,
it is beyond, with those who dwell in Your house,
that I will sing songs to You, in the innermost of
heaven.
My heart rises;
I fix my eyes upon You,
next to You, beside You,
O Giver of Life!   [14:133]

As Angel Garibay tells us, "el enigma de la muerte, inevitable y única, hemos visto poner sus sombras en todo canto de Anáhuac. Como si la obsesión del morir, elevado por el mito a la calidad de acto sacrificial, fuera la mayor que abrumaba aquellas conciencias" [10:I,195]. This obsession with death quite naturally reflected itself in ancient Nahuatl literature, and the cult of death which we see reflected today in contemporary Mexican literature is, without a doubt, at least in part, the result of and a holdover from this ancient, indigenous obsession.

The indigenous factor, though, is not the only one to be considered in determining the bases of what is referred to today as the "Mexican cult of death." The influence of the Christian death cult as brought to Mexico by the conquering Spaniards must not be ignored, nor minimized, if one is to provide a truly accurate panorama of the historical and literary bases of the Mexican cult of death.

Nuestras vidas son las ríos
que van a dar en la mar
que es el morir.

Jorge Manrique

The thought of death, which is thirst for immortality, is the profound concern of the Spanish people.

V. S. Pritchett

2

Historical and Literary Bases of the Cult of Death in Spain

With the coming of the Spanish conquistador, the Mexican cult of death began slowly to evolve into the phenomenon which we see reflected in Mexican literature and customs today. The Spanish Catholic brought with him to the New World a Christian death cult that, in many respects, was strikingly similar to its pagan counterpart, though the basic concepts of death of these two cultures may have differed rather significantly.

The historical bases of the cult of death in Spain are far more diverse and complex than those of the Mexican phenomenon; the roots of the Spanish character, of which the cult of death is an outstanding feature, lie not only in the indigenous Iberian culture, but also in the various other cultures that over the centuries have been imposed upon that area which is today Spain. In addition to the indigenous culture, the Germanic, the Semitic, and the Arabic cultures each contributed to a certain extent to the development of the Spanish cult of death. The Greek historian Strabo, for example, long ago observed, as a marked characteristic of the Iberian, an apparent delight in suffering and death. It is an aspect of the Iberian character to which scholars and historians have alluded consistently over the centuries. As Havelock Ellis observes, "when we reflect on the history of Spain and the temperament of the Spaniard, it is difficult not to realize a certain indifference to pain, almost a love of it. The early Iberians, even when nailed to the cross, still chanted their national songs, unvanquished in

21

spirit, to the astonishment of their Roman conquerors, and the Iberian mothers dashed their children to death rather than that they should live to be slaves" [15:43].

The centuries during which Spain pertained to the Roman Empire marked the occurrence of several events also significant to the development of the Spanish cult of death. Among these is the famous and much admired mass suicide at Sagunto in 219 B. C. , when the chief men of that city, allies of Rome, threw themselves and their treasures into the flames rather than surrender to the Carthaginians. It was an act that has been emulated many times in Spain's history.

These were also the years in which Seneca developed the stoic philosophy which is so closely associated with the cult of death and which for the Spaniards merely "answered to an instinct they already felt in their veins" [15:46].

In the subsequent discussion of the cult of death, as manifested in the contemporary Mexican short story, we will see that this stoic attitude, which was, and is, an outstanding characteristic of the Spaniard, found its counterpart in Mexico and, due to the resulting fusion of these two similar attitudes, was even further intensified there. As Joseph Velez explains, "La raza mexicana ha sido, y es, estoico por naturaleza. La actitud estoica se manifestaba ya antes de la Conquista cuando los indios eran sacrificados. Ahora que si se añade a esta actitud estoica de los españoles, se verá que la actitud azteca se refina y se manifiesta en una manera más prominente, y así ocurre" [16:46-47].

The entrance of Germanic tribes into Spain in A. D. 409 marked the beginning of a new step in Spanish history and a very significant one in the history of the cult of death. It was the Visigoths who, with the conversion of Recaredo in 589, adopted Catholicism and introduced the ecclesiastic culture into Spain. From that time on, Catholicism and the cult of death went hand in hand in Spain, for the Catholic Church provided the Spaniard with a philosophy which was delightfully compatible with his inherent fascination with death. We may trace most of the outstanding elements of the cult of death to the religious tenets of Catholicism, the contempt for terrestrial life and material values, the belief in an eternal life after death and the emphasis on the spiritual rather than the material, the preoccupation with the brevity of life and the mercurial nature of temporality, mortal corruption, and the idea of life as a dream. In short, a tendency appeared to put a far higher value on death or, rather, life after death than on life itself.

Thus, in the works of Miguel de Unamuno, one of Spain's outstanding intellectuals, one can readily discern the powerful influence of religious teachings and philosophy upon the Spanish attitude toward life and death.

> A human soul is worth all the universe, someone has said—
> I know not who, but it was excellently well said. A human
> soul, mind you! Not a human life. Not this life. [17:198]

> The Preacher's vision of life's tragedy caught the essential
> fact that everything is a dream. This "breath of Solomonic
> wisdom" was infused into the Spanish mentality, along with
> "a certain cult of vivifying death." The result was a kind of
> popular philosophy whose central idea was "the sense of
> the nothingness of everything temporal before the eternal,"
> a notion which "gives to our people a fortitude that shields
> them against the attacks of life." [18:269]

And, finally, speaking of the Spanish cult of death, he tells us,

> And what has been the deepest wellspring of the life of our
> nation but the longing to survive? For our so-called cult of
> death is nothing else. It is not our cult of death, but our cult
> of immortality. [19:171]

During the seven centuries after the defeat of the Visigoths in A. D. 711, two new cultures were introduced into Spain, the Arabic and the Hebrew. Their influence was such that, as Angel del Río states, "algunos reyes de Castilla, a partir de Alfonso VI, ostentan orgullosamente el título de 'Rey de las tres religiones'" [20:1,29].

The influence upon the cult of death of these cultures cannot compare, however, to that exerted by the Visigoths with the introduction of Catholicism into Spain. Catholicism was, and remains, by far the outstanding vehicle for expression of the cult of death in the Spanish world. But the Arabs and the Jews also exerted a certain influence upon the development of the phenomenon and may well have contributed significantly to its intensification. As Joseph Velez points out, "la influencia de los moros, influencia oriental-africana, se manifestó en las artes y en todos los aspectos de la vida española; especialmente en la actitud hacia la vida y hacia la muerte" [16:8].

The Spaniard's fatalistic nature, which will also be discussed at further length in subsequent chapters, has also been attributed to the Arabic strain in his blood, though I am inclined to agree with scholars who trace its origins to times considerably prior to the years of Arabic domination in Spain.

The Semitic influence upon the Spanish cult of death is essentially an indirect one in that it is in the books of the Old Testament prophets that one finds the roots of the profound Spanish preoccupation with the *vanitas-vanitatum* theme, despite the fact that these teachings and prophecies reached the Spanish people through the Catholic Church and not through Judaism. Also, the *amargo-vivir* sentiment, which Américo Castro sees as "característica del hispano-hebreo" [21:525], lends itself very well to the cult of death and may well have influenced later Christian literary production in Spain, in which manifestations of the phenomenon were clearly evident.

Basically these are the cultures and religions that together form the historical bases of the cult of death in Spain. The phenomenon was manifest in almost every aspect of Spanish life and culture. As was the case in Mexico, so, too, in Spain the artistic production of the nation reflected the preoccupation of her artists with the theme of death. "In Spanish painting and sculpture, the theme of death is treated again and again by every artist. The gloom of the mortuary, the luxury of the lying in state, is their favorite subject. The preoccupation is common in Catholic art, but no Catholic artists in other countries have had so exclusive a passion; it appears, also, in nonreligious painting" [22:66-67].

The phenomenon was also vigorously reflected in the nation's literary production. In discussing the manifestations of the cult of death in pre-Conquest Spanish literature, I shall confine my discussion again to poetry and endeavor to compare and contrast the manifestations of the death cult in Spanish poetry to those in Nahuatl poetry whenever possible, hoping, in this manner, to make apparent the fusion of certain elements from both cultures in the development of the death cult and its frequent manifestations in contemporary Mexican literature. "De siempre nos ha llamado la atención la repetida insistencia con que el tema de la muerte aflora en la literatura castellana. Hasta tal punto se manifiesta en todas las épocas que, sin temor a errar, podríamos calificarla como una de las 'constantes' del espíritu español. De una forma mas o menos ostensible, mas o menos oculta y callada, el sentido de la muerte aparece en la pintura, en la escultura, en la tradición folklórica y en todas las manifestaciones de nuestro arte culto o popular" [23:7].

Scholars of every age have noted and accepted this inherent predilection toward the idea of death in Spain, and repeatedly they have tried to answer the question of its existence and to discover the bases of this especially Spanish predisposition, a key to the very essence of the Spanish soul and to its metaphysical foundation, which has been indelibly stamped upon its literature. In the Middle Ages, for example, death was a dominant obsession of the Spaniard. He was born under the curse of original sin, he lived in constant fear of death from hunger, battle, or pestilence, and he was doomed, even in the world to come, to suffer in the flesh the pangs of purgatory or the more enduring torments of hell. In consequence, he viewed death and its terrors with feelings alternating between fear and contempt, and he dwelt on the spectacle of corruption with fascination [24:88-89].

In literature the salient motifs which gave expression to this obsession were essentially three in number. These, as expressed by the noted historian of the Middle Ages, J. Huizinga, were as follows: "The first is expressed by the question: Where are all those who once filled the world with their splendor? The second motif dwells on the frightful spectacle of human beauty gone to decay. The third is the death dance, death dragging along men of all conditions and ages" [25:193]. Of the three, Huizinga finds that in the Middle Ages the dance-of-death, or death-the-leveler, motif and the gruesome vision of mortal corruption were by far more potent than the elegiac ubi-sunt motif.

Toward the middle of the fourteenth century, we see these motifs displayed in one of the most famous works of the Spanish Middle Ages, *El libro de buen amor*, by Juan Ruiz, el Arcipreste de Hita. Death is not the principal theme in this work, but it is a conspicuous one in "La muerte de Trotaconventos" (stanzas 1520-75) and in the old woman's short epitaph which follows in stanzas 1576-78.

> Muerte, al que tú fieres, liévaslo de belmez;   1521
> al bueno e al malo. al noble e al rehez,
> a todos los egualas e lievas por un prez;
> por papas e por reys non das una vii nuez.
>
> Non catas señorio, debdo nin amistad;   1522
> con todo el mundo tienes cotiana enamistad;
> non ay en ti mesura, amor nin piadad,
> sinon dolor e tristeza, pena. e grand crueldad . . . .
>
> Dexas el cuerpo yermo a gusanos en fuessa;   1524
> al alma que lo puebla liévastela de priessa;
> non es el omne cierto de tu carrera aviessa;
> de fablar en ti, Muerte, espanto me atraviessa . . . .
>
> Fazes al mucho rico yazer en grand pobreza,   1528
> non tiene una meaja de toda su riqueza;
> el que bivo es bueno e de mucha nobleza,
> vil, fediondo es muerto, aborrida vileza . . . .
>
> Desprecias Ioçanía, el oro escureces,   1549
> desfazes la fechura, alegria entristeces,
> Manzillas la limpieza, cortesia envileces:
> Muerte, matas la vida, el amor aborreces . . . .
>
> Prendióme sin sospecha la Muerte en sus redes;   1577
> parientes e amigos, aquí non me acorredes;
> obrad bien en la vida. a Dios non lo erredes:
> que bien como yo morí, assí todos morredes.   [26:408-22]

It is plainly evident in these passages that in presenting a picture of medieval Spanish society, especially its more ribald aspects, Ruiz has not ignored the medieval Spaniard's obsession with death, and his influence upon future works in which the death theme will be an important, if not the exclusive, element is immense. As Juan Ayuso Rivera pointed out, "Se llega a través de toda la creación popular y anónima con notas de verdadera crudeza realista—como subraya Salinas—a la primera forma

expresa de elegía, dedicada a Trotaconventos por el propio Arcipreste:
'¡Ay muerte, muerte seas, muerte y malandante!'

"Esto va a señalar el nacimiento de toda una serie de Plantos,
Defunciones, Decires, Coplas. como los numerosos del Cancionero de
Baena" [23:98].

El libro de buen amor, then, provides us with one of the first
manifestations in literature of the Spanish cult of death. Even at this
early stage of development of the death theme, though, we notice
many similarities between this and the Nahuatl expression of the same
theme, and we also notice here the basic differences in concept and
interpretation of death which will ever distinguish these literatures one
from the other. One expression of the death theme that we find in both
literatures is that of the democratizing force of death, the idea that all
persons and things shall eventually have to face death regardless of their
social or economic status. We see this idea expressed often in *El libro de
buen amor*. Note, for example, stanzas 1521, 1522, and 1549. And we
see the same idea expressed in Nahuatl poetry, as, for example, in the
following poem written in ironic praise of King Itzcóatl:

> ¡Con este canto es la marcha
> a la región del misterio!
> Eres festejado,
> divinas palabras hiciste,
> ¡Pero has muerto! . . .
> Por eso cuando recuerdo a Itzcóatl,
> la tristeza invade mi corazón.
> ¿Es que estaba ya cansado?
> ¿O venció la pereza al Señor de la casa?
> El Dador de la vida a nadie hace resistente . . .
> Por esto continúa el cortejo:
> ¡es la marcha general!   [27:117]

Here, though, we also notice one of the fundamental differences
between these two concepts of death. In pre-Conquest Spanish poetry,
this democratizing force has not only physical implications, but also
moral ones. Ruiz, for example, not only warns us that all men and
things are subject to physical destruction, but he also warns us that
every man, despite his worldly status, may run the risk of eternal

damnation if he is not ever preparing himself for death by doing good works. In this respect, the pre-Conquest Mexican concept of death was less democratic, since paradise was reserved for only a select few.

As mentioned in the preceding chapter, the doctrine of Quetzalcóatl did contain certain laws of interior preparation which seemed to indicate that behavior in life was of some consequence for the soul, but these laws were completely corrupted by the Aztecs until only the manner of a man's death bore any significance in determining his soul's destination. But nowhere in any Mexican religion did there exist the concepts of heaven and hell that exist in Christendom. The idea that man could escape death through good works would have been inconceivable for the pre-Conquest Mexican. It was only a relatively small number of these people[2] who could expect anything other than a journey to Mictlan and eternal nothingness, and these achieved a different fate only by virtue of their manner of death and not by virtue of any moral conduct in life. Therefore, the fundamental difference between the views of death that existed for Spanish and Nahuatl cultures as manifested in their literatures was that, for the former, the preoccupation with the idea of death seemed to stem from an attempt to escape from it through salvation, whereby, for the other, this preoccupation seemed to stem from a natural bitterness, fascination, or intellectual curiosity resulting from confrontation with and acceptance of death as part of the natural order of existence.

---

2   The soldier who died in battle or on the sacrificial stone became a companion of the sun. His hours were filled with war songs and mock battles until, after four years. He was reincarnated as a hummingbird, flying from flower to flower in the warm air. Women who died in childbirth became goddesses and accompanied the sun from zenith to setting. For those who had died of drowning or by lightning or of a disease thought to be brought about by water, such as dropsy, Tlaloc, the Rain God, had reserved a tropical paradise filled with flowers and warm rain and peaceful happiness. For the rest there was Mictlan and a four-year journey through the underworld besieged by icy winds and monsters until they finally crossed the nine rivers into Hades and vanished totally and forever. [1:107-8]

To try to escape this natural order was inconceivable. As R. A. M. VanZantwijk explains it, "The West European wishes to be reminded as little as possible of the concept 'death' and he imagines his own family dead even as living beings (angels) in order, nevertheless, to escape being confronted with the hard truth of death. The Aztecs perceive life and death as indivisibly bound up together, and as such the one is not preferable to the other. The contradistinction which Europeans see between life and death does not arise in the Aztec train of thought. In Europe life is connected with beauty and death, with the lugubrious, the hideous; the Aztecs see only the beauty of the natural order in which life and death appear as indivisible components of progress" [7:75]. Thus, nowhere in Nahuatl literature do we find anything that approximates the moralizing tone present in Ruiz's passages on death and characteristic of Spanish moralistic poetry in general, for, just as this moralizing tone is characteristic of the pre-Conquest cult of death in Spanish literature, the lack of it is characteristic of the Nahuatl.

Also, along these same lines, we might note that the view of death presented by Juan Ruiz is, in general, a far more negative one than any we find in Nahuatl poetry. This again is most assuredly due to the fact that the Christian believed in the possibility of escape from death and, therefore, viewed it as something completely negative, synonymous in his mind with all that is vile, evil, and fearsome. Death was viewed as the end of all things, not as a part of a natural cyclical order of existence. It is "dolor e tristeza, pena e grand crueldad" (1522), and he who dies "vil, fediondo es muerto. aborrida vileza" (1528).

Though the fear of death is natural to all human beings, it is expressed in Nahuatl literature most often as a lament for the futility of life—an idea unheard of for the Christian, who saw life as a trial which everyone must undergo to achieve eternal life—or, in the tone of a question, as a search for the truth of what was and what would be—also out of the question for the Christian, whose religion provided him with a clear statement of the meaning of life and a detailed picture of life after death either in heaven or in hell. Nowhere in Nahuatl literature do we find the gruesome vision of mortal corruption, of worms and decay, that we see in Ruiz and in the works of many later writers. Nor would we find reference to the abhorrent physical nature of the dead in the literature of a people who were accustomed to the sight of human sacrifice, the taste of human flesh, and the veneration of death objects in their art and in their everyday lives.

The essential difference in literary expression of the death theme between the Nahuatl and the Spanish, even in its earliest stages of development, is clearly the result of differing concepts of the nature of death. For the Spaniard it was a vile and ugly phenomenon which could and ought to be escaped through salvation. For the ancient Mexican it was a natural phenomenon as much a part of life as life itself and devoid of any negative or positive implications such as heaven and hell. The concept of *libre albedrío*, or "free will," present in Ruiz and all moralistic poetry of pre-Conquest Spain and brought to its apogee in the works of Calderón de la Barca, is utterly lacking in Nahuatl poetry.

Half a century after the creation of *El libro de buen amor*, *La danza de la muerte* appeared. The medieval obsession with death is here painful and terrifying, and the didactic purpose of the poem is evident: to emphasize that everyone must one day face death, often an unexpected one, and that he should be ever avoiding sin or he may face eternal damnation. The poem is in the form of a vast allegory, forerunner of the more sophisticated *autos sacramentales* of the Golden Age, in which Death describes herself in all of her ugliness and calls people of various ages and social stations to join in her macabre dance.

> Yo soy la muerte cierta a todas criaturas
> que son y serán en el mundo durante;
> demando y digo: ¡Oh. honbre!. ¡Por qué curas
> de vida tan breve en punto pasante?
> Pues no hay tan fuerte ni recio gigante
> que de este mi arco se puede amparar,
> conviene que mueras cuando lo tirar
> con esta mi flecha cruel traspasante.
>
> A la danza mortal venid los nacidos
> que en el mundo sois de cualquier estado,
> el que no quisiere a fuerza y amidos
> hacerle he venir muy toste priado.
> Pues que ya el fraile os ha predicado
> que todos vayáis a hacer penitencia,

el que no quisiere poner diligencia
por mí no puede ser más esperado.   [28:143-44]

The outstanding motifs in this poem are the dance-of-death, death-the-leveler motif and the mortal-corruption motif. Here, as in *El libro de buen amor*, the emphasis is on the democratizing force of death and the transitory nature of beauty, wealth, and traditional, worldly values. Also analogous to *El libro de buen amor* are the strong social satire and the humor displayed in this work, though it must be noted that the humor in *La danza de la muerte* is of a far more macabre nature than that of *El libro de buen amor*, and its degree and purpose far less open to discussion.

Here we might notice another parallel between the Spanish and Nahuatl where both use poetry as a means of social protest. In the Nahuatl we see an example of this in the poem to King Itzcóatl, cited earlier in this chapter.

During the early fifteenth century, the dance-of-death, death-the-leveler, and mortal-corruption motifs were carried on by didactic poets with little variation from the manner in which their fourteenth-century predecessors had used them as a warning to their pleasure-loving contemporaries. The *canciller* Pero López de Ayala, whose work was to greatly influence moralistic poetry for the next half century, in an early part of his *Rimado de Palacio*, presents the death-the-leveler theme in the following manner:

Bien sabes tu, por çierto, e non deues dudar.
Ca la muerte non sabe a ninguno perdonar,
A grandes e pequeños, todos quiere matar,
E todos en comun por ella han de pasar.   [29:1,94]

As flagrant corruption and striving for wealth came to characterize the reign of Juan II, the dance-of-death, death-the-leveler motif gained new power and social significance, becoming an indispensable element in didactic poems of the period.

Hand in hand with this motif was that of mortal corruption, the loathsome vision of bodily decay and decomposition which so effectively struck fear in the hearts of the people of those times. Echoing

the warning tone of the biblical prophets, López de Ayala created the
following lines of his *Rimado de Palacio*:

> El vno enrriqueçe, al otro va muy mal;
> Despues viene la muerte, que a todos es egual,
> E los cubren gusanos e cosas non les ual . . .   [29: 1,128]

Sánchez Talavera uses the same theme in a *deçir* composed at the
death of Ruy Díaz de Mendoza when, recalling certain prominent
figures carried off by death, he states,

> Todos aquestos que aqui son nombrados,
> los vnos son fechos çenisa e nada,
> los otros son huesos la carne quitada
> e son derramados por los fonssados;
> los otros estan ya descoyuntados
> cabeças syn cuerpos, syn pies e syn manos;
> los otros comiençan comer los gusanos,
> los otros acaban de ser enterrados.   [30: III, 1076]

The mortal-corruption motif also commonly took the form of a
lament for feminine beauty. Note, for example, the following stanzas
from *La danza de la muerte*, in which Death calls two young maidens
to her dance.

> A éstas y a todos por las posturas
> daré fealdad la vida partida,
> y desnudedad por las vestiduras,
> por siempre jamás muy triste aburrida;
> y por los palacios daré por medida
> sepulcros oscuros de dentro hedientes,
> y por los manjares gusanos royentes
> que coman de dentro su carne podrida.   [28:144]

References of this type to the transitory nature of physical beauty
were frequent in pre-Conquest Spanish poetry. And we see something
of this same sort in Nahuatl poetry, though such references therein are
achieved through comparisons of man to nature— man as the flowers,

for example—rather than through graphic descriptions of physical deterioration.

The *ubi-sunt* motif, as we have seen, was generally far less popular during the fourteenth century than were the dance-of-death and mortal-corruption motifs. During the fifteenth century, however, this motif enjoyed a noteworthy revival, presaged at the turn of the century by López de Ayala's *Rimado de Palacio*.

A conventional element of the ubi-sunt motif, particularly popular in the fifteenth century and also evident in Nahuatl poetry, was the catalogue of illustrious personages of antiquity. Of this device we see an excellent example in the following *deçir* by Gonzalo Martínez de Medina, whose catalogue progressively moves from the great mythical and historical figures of antiquity to those of contemporary Spain:

> Mira que fue del grande greçiano
> Alixandre, Julio e Dario e Pompeo,
> Hercoles, Archiles, don Ector troyano,
> Priamo e Mino e Judas Macabeo,
> Dandolo, Trabo, Suero e Tolomeo,
> Menbrot, Golias, el fuerte Sanson,
> Vergilio, Aristotiles, el gran Godeon,
> e todos los otros que en los libros leo . . . .
>
> Mira el d'Estuniga e el de Velasco
> que ayer estauan en muy grand potençia,
> e como sus fijos avien d'ellos asco
> despues que la muerte mostro su presençia;
> ¿que pro les touo la grand exçelençia
> nin rricos thesoros tan mal allegados,
> castillos e villas, baxillas, estados,
> que asy poseyeron con tanta femençia?
> [30:11,749]

Two other elements commonly combined within the *ubi-sunt* motif were social satire and the melancholy *vanitas-vanitatum*. Together these two created a tone of warning reminiscent of the Old Testament prophets.[3] The inevitable similes of life as a dream, a flower, a river, and a passing breeze recur frequently in passages of this type. This emphasis on the mercurial nature of temporality, with its underlying tone of warning, weaves thread-like throughout the poetry of the fifteenth century, from Ayala to Manrique.

> Non es segurança en cosa que sea,
> Que todo es sueño e flor que peresçe,
> el rico, el pobre, quando bien se otea,
> conosçe qu'es viento e pura sandeçe; . . .
> [30:11,764]

> Las justas y los torneos,
> paramentos. bordaduras
> y cimeras,
> ¿fueron sino devaneos?
> ¿que fueron sino verduras
> de las eras? . . .
> ¿dónde iremos a buscallos?
> ¿que fueron sino rocíos
> de los prados?
> [28:172]

It is here that we find one of the most marked similarities between Spanish and Nahuatl poetry, for not only do we find the same emphasis on temporality, but we also find a strikingly similar use of imagery in the two poetries. For example, in the Spanish poems presented above, we note the prevalence of the similes of life as a dream and life, or man, as the flowers. A marked propensity toward the same similes is evident in the following Nahuatl poem:

---

3   ''Etienne Gilson en 'Les idees et les lettres' ha seguido la trayectoria de esta preocupación profunda por cantar la brevedad de las cosas terrenas, y encuentra las fuentes mas antiguas en Baruc (111,16-20), el Eclesiastes e Isaias'' [23:99].

Sólo venimos a dormir, sólo venimos a soñar:
no es verdad, no es verdad que venimos a vivir en la tierra.

En yerba de primavera venimos a convertirnos:
llegan a reverdecer, llegan a abrir sus corolas
nuestros corazones.
es una flor nuestro cuerpo: da algunas flores y se seca.
[12:31]

The preoccupation with the brevity of life and the mercurial nature of temporality is, therefore, typical of both Nahuatl and Spanish poetry, both exhibiting a strikingly similar use of imagery to express this preoccupation. We would never find in Spanish poetry, as we do in the Nahuatl, the comparison of a sacrificial victim to a flower or a popular expression of the inanity of life, which in the Nahuatl is often linked with the obsession with its brevity, but we do find a definite tendency in both literatures toward melancholy. In studies of both cultures, this melancholic nature has been related to the cult of death.

Finally, there are two other elements in both pre-Conquest literatures which are of significant interest in the discussion of the cult of death. The first of these is the glorification of the soldier's death, the Spanish *buena muerte*. For both cultures, with their traditional cults of fame and stoic natures, this type of death signified everlasting renown and heavenly reward. Thus, in the Nahuatl, poems of this nature, the *cantos de águilas, de príncipes, de guerra*, constitute an entire category of lyric poetry. Of these we saw several examples in the preceding chapter. And in the Spanish, examples of poetry in praise of the *buena muerte* also abound and are particularly noticeable in the poetry of the various illustrious members of Jorge Manrique's family, as in the following section of the *Proverbios* of the Marqués de Santillana and in the last part of Manrique's Coplas:

Codro quiso mas vençer
que non biuir;
non refuso morir
e padesçer
por ganar e non perder
noble conpaña:

35

buen morir es por fazaña
de fazer.
[32;446-47]

Y pues vos, claro varón,
tanta sangre derramásteis
de paganos,
esperad el galardón
que en este mundo ganásteis
por las manos;
y con esta confianza,
y con la fe tan entera
que tenéis,
partid con buena esperanza,
que est a otra vida tercera
ganaréis.
[28:175]

Anna Krause refers to the cult of fame as "the most vital adjustment which the Spaniard of the fifteenth century made to the problem of death, . . . the rational and heroic adjustment which enabled the more advanced minds of the period to rise above the negative aspect of death" [31:121, 124]. This they did to the point whereby death, the traditional epitome of all that was ugly and vile, was actually clothed in beauty. The parallel between Spanish and Nahuatl poetry as it concerns this particular element of the cult of death is very nearly exact.

Hand in hand with this glorification of the *buena muerte* was the consolatory element, cultivated with special predilection in Spanish poetry by Gómez Manrique. This poetic genre, which preached the stoic acceptance of the death of a loved one, relieved at last of life's trials, "urges Christian fortitude in accepting the *breves amarguras* of this life that we may enjoy the delights of the hereafter. The stoic and the Christian note are thus fused in characteristic manner" [31:121]. Obviously the Christian element in this type of poetry would be lacking in the Nahuatl; nonetheless, the stoic element was emphatically present in much of Nahuatl poetry. Stoicism in the face of the death of a loved one was encouraged to such an extent in Aztec Mexico that there actually existed a law prohibiting any obvious display of grief over the sacrifice of one's child. Any negative reaction to human sacrifice at all carried with it the strong possibility of punishment by death.

Let us again consider the Spanish ideology. If we regard literature, in this case poetry, as the reflection of the subconscious of its author, who is in turn the product of his culture, it seems that the preceding references to the three motifs, dance-of-death/death-the-leveler, mortal-corruption, and *ubi-sunt*, and their obvious popularity in pre-Conquest literature, as well as the popularity of the consolatory genre and the glorification of the *buena muerte*, must indicate a definite preoccupation with death in pre-Conquest Spain. To quote again J. Huizinga, "no other epoch has laid so much stress as the expiring Middle Ages on the thought of death. An everlasting call of *memento mori* resounds through life" [25:138]. This statement seems to find strong literary support in the literature of pre-Conquest Spain. Throughout Spanish literature, examples in every century attest to the fact that this Spanish preoccupation with death did not end with the Conquest. It went on to flourish in that century and in the following one under such exemplary poets as the sixteenth-century mystics and the great poets of the seventeenth century, among whom, in regard to the use of the death theme, loom prominent the figures of Quevedo and Calderón. It continued through the Romantics, the Naturalists, and into the twentieth century until, discussing the poetry of García Lorca, Pedro Salinas is moved to say, "Pero Lorca, aunque expresa con originalidad y acento personal evidentes el mismo sentir de la muerte, no ha tenido que buscarlo por procesos de especulación interior, en las galerías de su alma. Se lo encuentra en torno suyo, en el aire natal donde alienta, en los cantares de las servidoras de su casa, en los libros de su lengua, en las iglesias de su tierra; se lo encuentra en todo lo que su persona individual tiene de pueblo, de herencia secular. Nace Lorca en un país que lleva siglos viviendo un especial tipo de cultura, el que llamo 'cultura de la muerte' "[33:374].

La muerte calaca y flaca—
  no engorda por mas que empaca.

Popular refrain

3

The Cult of Death as a Social Phenomenon

PATRICK ROMANELL, in *Making of the Mexican Mind*, presents a very effective comparison of the North American and Mexican mentalities. Franklin D. Roosevelt's phrase "rendezvous with Destiny," he tells us, "suits perfectly a people like ours, ever confident of achieving bigger and better things, material and spiritual. And were we to compare the other America's mentality with ours, the corresponding phrase which comes closest to revealing her tragic sense of life would be that of Mexico-inspired American poet Alan Seeger, 'rendezvous with Death' "[34:24].

Pre-Conquest Nahuatl culture and pre-Conquest Spanish culture together form the soil in which the roots of modern Mexican society grew and were nurtured over the centuries. The bases of the Mexican cult of death clearly lie in these cultures. But just as a child is born of his parents and grows to be an individual distinct from either of his progenitors, so the contemporary Mexican cult of death developed into a phenomenon significantly distinct from either of those from which it was born. As Octavio Paz points out, "la muerte mexicana es estéril, no engendra como la de aztecas y cristianos" [35:49].

The centuries that followed the Conquest and the confrontation of indigenous and Spanish cultures saw their gradual fusion into one culture distinct from either of them, yet containing elements of both. Death as a way of life was an element inherited from both mother cultures and sustained by four centuries following the Conquest in which "Mexico experienced more violence to life than any other country in the world" [36:3]. "The colonial era was one of slow attrition and of relative peace, during which the blood and culture of conquering Spain, imposed on the native Indian masses, fused and faded into an ethnic and cultural pattern that after 300 years emerged definitely Mexican in stamp and spirit" [89:xxxiv]. During this period of "relative peace," however, over 7 million members of the indigenous population perished violently or from imported disease, until, almost 300 years later, on September 16, 1810, an outcry was heard in the village of Dolores, Guanajuato, that was to initiate a series of revolutions and outbreaks which would last intermittently for over a century and which would put an end to the colonial era in Mexico. For over half a century thereafter, Mexico was wracked by war with foreign enemies and by internal strife between the warring liberal and conservative factions of the government. The Porfirio Díaz regime brought with it a period of unequaled prosperity and peace (based upon absolute suppression). By the end of this regime, the Revolution of 1910 was imminent.

The Mexican Revolution of 1910, "the only true revolution Mexico has ever had" [89:xxxvi-vii], was directed solely against the unconstitutional Díaz regime and at its outset displayed no clear-cut program for social reform. It was only after seven years of bloody contention among the various revolutionary leaders that the ideals for which the Revolution has come to stand were formulated and given official form in the Constitution of 1917.

In the two and a half decades following the outbreak of the Revolution, Mexico knew little real peace. By 1928 all of the major revolutionary leaders had been killed and a Catholic rebellion had taken place. It was not until late 1931 and the inauguration of Lázaro Cárdenas as president that Mexico began to acquire a certain amount of stability and embark upon the road to lasting peace. Since then, instances of mass violence have been on the decline, but centuries of violence have left their stamp on all aspects of Mexican life and letters, constituting an outstanding element of the New Mexican society.

As we know, literature is often the reflection of the subconscious of its author who is, in turn, the product of his culture or society. It is most important, therefore, that we define the cult of death as a social phenomenon before going on to the discussion of its manifestations in literature. Consequently, the views of several leading scholars of contemporary Mexican culture are presented in an attempt to demonstrate clearly and definitively what is meant by the term "cult of death."

In *Six Faces of Mexico*, Russell C. Ewing states that "everywhere in the worship of the gods, in the processes of village government, in the dances and other arts, there has been and still continues a fusion of Indian and European. These mixed ways of rural life and in a large part of city life—these blends of cultural traditions—are the essential Mexico. It is often hard to tell which tradition is dominant, if either" [37:66].

As some of the prominent manifestations of the cult of death in contemporary Mexican society are reviewed, the reader should keep in mind that most of them are products of this process of fusion. For example, from their indigenous heritage of human sacrifice and of complete disregard for the individual, from their utter defeat at the hands of the Spaniards, which in their minds could only have been explainable as an act of "traición de los dioses, que reniegan de su pueblo" [35:46], and, finally, from the pitiful decimation of their people to one-seventh of the original population in a mere thirty years following the Conquest, comes the deep sense of inferiority of the Mexicans, which, in turn, leads to "fantasies in which one is a hero or a saint" [38:218]. And to become either, one must die. Therefore, one of the outstanding proofs of a man's virility in modern Mexico is "cuando afirma convincentemente o demuestra que no le tiene miedo a la muerte" [39:15]. "Death is the ultimate means to salvage prestige. The fondness for dying—Iturriaga calls it necrolatry—seems rooted in both the indigenous civilization and in Spanish culture" [38:219], in the deified sacrificial victim, but also in the Spaniard with his profound and often suicidal cult of fame. Undoubtedly from these same sources stems the ever-popular Mexican maxim, "Dime cómo mueres y te diré quién eres" [35:45].

The Mexican's attitude toward death, his indifference toward it as well as his fascination with it, is very effectively explained in the following passages by Octavio Paz who, better than any scholar today, has brought to light the true nature of the Mexican soul.

> La indiferencia del mexicano ante la muerte se nutre de su indiferencia ante la vida. . . .Nuestras canciones, refranes, fiestas y reflexiones populares manifiestan de una manera inequívoca que la muerte no nos asusta porque "la vida nos ha curado de espantos." Morir es natural y hast a deseable, cuanto más pronto, major. . . .Matamos porque la vida, la nuestra y la ajena, carece de valor. Y es natural que así ocurra: vida y muerte son inseparables y cada vez que la primera pierde significación, la segunda se vuelve intrascendente. . . .Ante ambas el mexicano se cierra, las ignora. . . . [Sin embargo, la muerte] está presente en nuestras fiestas, en nuestros juegos, en nuestros amores y en nuestros pensamientos. Morir y matar son ideas que pocas veces nos abandonan. La muerte nos seduce . . . . La muerte nos atrae. Por otra parte, la muerte nos venga de la vida, la desnuda de todas sus vanidades y pretensiones y la convierte en lo que es: unos huesos mondos y una mueca espantable. En un mundo cerrado y sin salida, en donde todo es muerte, lo único valioso es la muerte.
> [35:48-49]

It is not surprising, then, that in a test undertaken to measure the degree of perturbation caused by each of 100 selected words, the word "death" fell into the fifth, or minimum, range of perturbation among Mexican women tested and into the fourth range, also very low, among Mexican men [40:47].

Finally, a much noted psychological manifestation of the cult of death is the Mexican's strikingly fatalistic and stoic nature. "El estoicismo ante el dolor y la muerte" and "un sentimiento de pesimismo en el fondo del alma" [41:122, 123] were fundamental characteristics of the Aztec personality. The "famous fatalism of the race" [42:32]. ascribable both to the Arabic strain in their ancestry and to an innate religious disposition, as well as Senecan stoicism, "the fundamental philosophy and almost religion of Spain" [15:45], were fundamental characteristics of the Spaniards. As Joseph Velez points out, "un pueblo fatalista y lleno de ideas lúgubres y fúnebres, por causa de su religión, unirá su sangre y su civilización a un pueblo igualmente fatalista y estoico por causa, también de su religion. El resultado de esta fusión ya se puede adivinar sin necesidad de ser determinista" [16:14]. The result was that Aztec attitudes were refined and augmented by their Christian counterparts until they manifested themselves in a manner more prominent than either of these.

Physical manifestations of the Mexican's attitude toward death also abound in his everyday life and customs. A few of these that I have noted in my own travels in Mexico are the exceedingly sanguinary religious statuary displayed in Mexican churches—Christ, the suffering Savior, streaming with blood and clothed in gaping wounds; martyred saints graphically displaying their wounds—and the real or simulated remains of various saints, church dignitaries, or Christ Himself, presented for the viewing in glass-topped coffins, often wrapped in blood-stained gauze, in very many Mexican churches. Also conspicuous is the presence of skulls, skeletons, mummies, or other death objects of one material or another in virtually every Mexican household and the presence of these same objects as part of the decorations applied by bus drivers to the front section of their vehicles. (Among which the most striking may be the doll's head so often appearing on the shift lever of the bus, usually as a handle.) Noteworthy, too, are the frequent allusions to death in the graffiti written on Mexican trucks. And, finally, Mexican newspapers display a definite talent for graphic detail in reporting traffic fatalities, murders, or other acts of violence, while black-bordered death notices are inordinately precise and scattered conspicuously throughout each newspaper. Another interesting manifestation of the cult of death that I have personally viewed is the mummies of Guanajuato. Here and in several other places in Mexico, the mummified remains of the dead are proudly displayed for all to see, as if to announce to the world that "el mexicano está acostumbrado a vivir codo con codo con la muerte y no la teme, antes por el contrario, la acepta y la acepta como su compañera" [16:36]. I was particularly surprised to learn from a guide with whom I discussed this rather gruesome display that the majority of the visitors to the catacombs in which the mummies are displayed are not foreign tourists, as would be expected, but, rather, Mexicans, either vacationers to the city or residents thereof. Apparently such a display is repulsive to many foreigners; certainly many Americans would find it so, but it has proven so popular among Mexicans that the mummies eventually had to be placed behind glass partitions to prohibit their being picked apart by tourists desirous of a souvenir of their visit.

Many other manifestations of the cult of death have been noted by scholars of Mexican culture. Tavera notes and substantiates with Rorschach records the "morbid eagerness" of Mexican medical students [43], while others have linked to the cult of death the bullfight, the machismo syndrome, and the high rate of homicide in Mexico, "the highest culpable homicide rate of the nations of the world that keep accurate records" [36:5]. The cult of death is also effectively reflected in Mexican sayings and jokes as, for example, in the following two jokes from A. Jímenez's *Picardía mexicana*:

> -¿Te gustan las flores?
> -Sí.
> -Bueno (saca su revólver y ipum, pum!),
> ¡que te lleven coronas!

> -Mira, ése es mi papá.
> -¿Cual?
> -El del sombrero de charro.
> -Los dos llevan sombrero de charro.
> -El de la camisa blanca.
> -Pero si los dos la traen blanca.
> -Te voy a indicar cual. (Apunta Y ¡pum, pum!)
> El que cae.   [44:230]

But the manifestation par excellence of the Mexican cult of death is the national celebration of the Day of the Dead on November 2. "Tan acostumbradas están las gentes a la presencia constante de la muerte que sus ritos y ceremonias son manifestaciones de su actitud" [16:35]. "Candies and pastries in the form of skulls, toy coffins, and funeral processions of paper figurines are among the many macabre playthings on sale for the festival" [38:219]. "Comemos el día de los Difuntos panes que fingen huesos y nos divierten canciones y chascarrillos en los que ríe la muerte pelona" [35:49]. In many parts of Mexico, specifically in those in which there is still a strong Indian tradition, this celebration, "a convenient adaptation of an ancient Indian Day of the Dead called Tzi kin" [45:88], is of a full month's duration, the greatest ceremony being on November 2. On this day, it is believed, the dead are permitted to come to earth to visit their relatives, partake of the spirit of food and gifts brought to them at their final resting places, and warm themselves over the candles and fires kept burning there. W. E. Garrett explains the ceremony as it takes place in the cemetery on Janitzio Island in Lake Pátzcuaro. "Shortly after midnight, on November 2, the island women bring to their family burial plots an assortment of gifts, food, candles, marigolds,[4] and wooden frames decorated with flowers, fruit and small skulls molded of sugar. They spread mats on the ground and set up the decorations—one candle for each remembered relative and a censer of burning copal. They arrange the food and sprinkle marigold petals over the entire setting. Then the women and children sit in contemplation or chant prayers throughout the chill night. . . .'Salga, salga, salga, . . .' a fisherman chanter implores a departed soul" [46:146, 181-85].

The cult of death was eloquently decribed by a poor Indian with no formal education who became the 1970s most popular and well-known Mexican "philosopher," Juan Matus, the *brujo* whose teachings inspired a series of best-selling volumes by Carlos Castaneda. Don Juan, as a "man of knowledge" and a living compendium of Mexican thought and culture, explains that

> By the time knowledge becomes a frightening affair, the man also realizes that death is the irreplaceable partner that sits next to him on the mat. Every bit of knowledge that becomes power has death as its central force. Death lends the ultimate touch, and whatever is touched by death indeed becomes power . . . .

> Thus, to be a warrior, a man has to be, first of all, and rightfully so, keenly aware of his own death. But to be concerned with death would force anyone of us to focus on the self, and that would be debilitating. So the next thing one needs to be a warrior is detachment. The idea of imminent death,

---

4   The marigold, it might be noted, called the "flower ofthe dead," is also a solar symbol, and, therefore, well attests to the dualistic nature of the celebration—that is, that it is a product of both pagan and Christian tradition

instead of becoming an obsession, becomes an indifference [47:182-83]

"How can anyone feel so important when we know that death is stalking us?" he asked . . . .
"The thing to do when you're impatient," he proceeded, "is to turn to your left and ask advice from your death. An immense amount of pettiness is dropped if your death makes a gesture to you, or if you catch a glimpse of it, or if you just have the feeling that your companion is there watching you. . . ."
He replied that the issue of our death was never pressed far enough. And I argued that it would be meaningless for me to dwell upon my death, since such a thought would only bring discomfort and fear.
"You're full of crap" he exclaimed. "Death is the only wise adviser that we have. Whenever you feel, as you always do, that everything is going wrong and you're about to be annihilated, turn to your death and ask if that is so. Your death will tell you that you're wrong, that nothing really matters outside its touch. Your death will tell you, 'I haven't touched you yet." [48:55]

From the discussion of the background and nature of the cult of death in Mexico and its early manifestations in literature, let us now turn to the other basic topic of consideration in this study, manifestations of the Mexican cult of death in the Mexican short story. In the following chapter, I will deal with several of the 20th century's outstanding authors of this genre.

Los seres humanos mueren todo el tiempo, a cada instante, en cada rincón. Al morir, al tener que morir, ya han muerto, ya recuerdan su muerte futura, anticipan su muerte pasada, mueren su vida presente.

Ariel Dorfman

True life nourishes itself on death and renews itself second by second, in a continuous creation. A life without any death in it, without any unpiling in its continual piling up, would be a perpetual death, the repose of a stone. Those who do not die do not live; those who do not die at every instant, to rise from the dead on the instant, do not live.

Unamuno

Todo al fin es muerte . . . distintos modos de morir.

Clara Passafari

4

Manifestations of the Cult of Death in the 20th Century Mexican Short Story

We have seen that the bases of the cult of death lie in both the pre-Conquest indigenous and the pre-Conquest Spanish cultures and that the result of the fusion of these cultures was that the cult of death became an even more prominent aspect of the new Mexican society, to the point where we find it still very much alive today and one of the outstanding social phenomena of contemporary Mexico. As would be expected, literary manifestations of the cult of death abound, not only in pre-Conquest Mexican and pre-Conquest Spanish literature, but also in the most recent works. As Aguiles Nazoa points out, "Entre los signos adversos a que algunos pueblos de América acogieron las expresiones de su animismo colectivo, ninguno iguala como poder omnipresente a ese sombrío Numen de todo lo mexicano, que se llama la Muerte" [49:163].

We have also observed that one of the newest and most successfully cultivated literary genres in Mexico is the short story and that many of the best writers of the country were, during the 20th century, turning their attention and talents to the cultivation of that genre which, according to Seymour Menton, "al cumplir cien años, ha llegado a tal grado de perfección que está en una meseta de la cual no se si va a seguir subiendo" [50:51]. Let us, therefore, turn our attention to a study of the manifestations of the cult of death in this powerful genre, the contemporary Mexican short story.

I have chosen to focus my discussion on the years 1947-60. During these years, there arose in Mexican literature a group of authors whose writings indicate a conscientious attempt on their part to uncover certain outstanding aspects of *mexicanidad* and, in some cases, to search out their roots in indigenous culture and to illustrate the degree to which ancient customs and attitudes have influenced the contemporary Mexican attitude toward life and death. Invariably in their attempt to uncover the Mexican soul, the authors had to deal with the cult of death.

In this chapter, we shall examine the manifestations of this phenomenon in the short stories of six authors, Juan Rulfo, José Revueltas, Rosario Castellanos, Guadalupe Dueñas, Carlos Fuentes, and Eraclio Zepeda. Of the six, several have achieved international renown and are considered among Mexico's most famous and skilled writers. Others have enjoyed considerable fame within Mexico. And all but the youngest of these have participated in the "Los narradores ante el publico" lecture series in Mexico City. They do differ, though, in the degree to which the short story has influenced the fame of each as a writer. José Revueltas, Rosario Castellanos, and Carlos Fuentes owe their fame primarily to the novel; yet, they have also written many excellent short stories and are generally included in the best collections of the genre. Guadalupe Dueñas and Eraclio Zepeda, on the other hand, owe their fame to the short story, while Juan Rulfo owes his fame equally to the short story and the novel, his entire literary production consisting of one outstanding work in each genre. There is no question that Juan Rulfo is one of Mexico's greatest writers of short stories. He is also the greatest single exponent of the cult of death in Mexican literature, a fact that is hardly surprising if we consider the following details of his personal history.

Rulfo is a native of Jalisco, the state in which each of his short stories is set; and, although some fellow writers and critics, such as Juan José Arreola, may express feelings to the contrary, the majority of critics seem to feel that his physical descriptions of the Jaliscan southwest are quite accurate. The cult of death manifested in his short stories is to some extent, then, a direct result of the physical environment in which Rulfo was born and raised. "The landscape . . . is decrepit. The living are surrounded by the dead . . .. Most people have migrated. Those who have stayed behind are there to keep the dead company.

'Their ancestors tie them to the place. They don't want to leave their dead.' Sometimes when they move, they actually dig up their graves. 'They carry their dead on their shoulders.' Even when they leave them behind, they continue to bear their weight" [51:249-50].

Rulfo himself is by no means free from this weight as is attested to by his obsession with tracing the genealogy of his family, a second point of interest in his personal history. A brief look at this genealogy suggests another motive for Rulfo's being such an outstanding literary spokesman for the Mexican cult of death, for lives of violence and early death abound in the Rulfo family tree. As Rulfo tells us,

> A mi padre no lo mató un peón, no tenía peones, y eso lo ha afirmado erróneamente Seymour Menton en su libro *La cuentística iberoamericana*. . . . Lo mataron una vez cuando huía . . . y a mi tío lo asesinaron, y a otro y a otro . . . y al abuelo lo colgaron de los dedos gordos, los perdió . . .todos morían a los treinta y tres años.
> [52: viii-ix]

> En la familia Perez Rulfo, nunca hubo mucha paz; todos morían temprano, a la edad de treinta y tres años y todos eran asesinados por la espalda. Sólo a David, el último, víctima de su afición, lo mató un caballo.
> [53:65]

From this family tradition and from the regional and national tradition of which it was a product, *El llano en llamas* was born, a collection of fifteen short stories published in 1953. Certainly death was a "constant companion" of Juan Rulfo as he wrote the stories of *El llano en llamas*. The setting, the characterization, and the action of each story is infused with manifestations of the cult of death. In some stories, however, one element—either setting, characterization, or action—manifests the phenomenon particularly well. I have chosen to discuss three short stories from the collection that I feel best utilize one of these elements as a vehicle of expression of the cult of death. These are, for its use of setting, "Luvina"; for characterization, "La Cuesta de las Comadres"; and for action, "El llano en llamas."

Richard M. Eastman, in *A Guide to the Novel,* makes the following observations concerning the setting of a fictional work: "Through the techniques of thematic or symbolic imagery, the novelist may select some physical detail of his story and so impregnate it with thematic associations that whenever that detail recurs, it embodies that theme" [54:59]. Juan Rulfo, in the stories of *El llano en llamas,* has made a microcosm of the Jaliscan southwest, and he has so impregnated that setting with thematic associations that it embodies the theme of death. The villages and the landscape depicted in these stories are, in the words of the author, "like graveyards dedicated to the cult of death" [51:266].

Among the fifteen stories of *El llano en llamas,* the example par excellence of Rulfo's use of setting as a vehicle of expression of the Mexican cult of death is "Luvina," the name of a village that is, in the words of the narrator, a onetime resident of the place, "el purgatorio. Un lugar moribundo donde se han muerto hasta los perros y ya no hay ni quien le ladre al silencio" [55:104]. Luvina is little more than a ghost town in which fertility has become sterility and from which the truly living have long ago fled, leaving behind only a small group of spectral, unhappy figures—bat-like figures who "pass by like shadows," "esposas sin maridos, . . . niños sin infancia, . . . viejos sentados en el umbral de las puertas, esperando la muerte" [56:48]—tied to their dead and themselves more dead than alive. Nothing lives in Luvina. A black mountain wind does not even let the dulcamaras grow, "esas plantitas tristes que apenas si pueden vivir un poco untadas a la tierra, agarradas con todas sus manos al despeñadero de los montes" [55:94]. "Todo el lomerío pelón, sin un árbol, sin una cosa verde para descansar los ojos; todo envuelto en el calín ceniciento. Usted verá eso: aquellos cerros apagados como si estuvieran muertos y a Luvina en el más alto, coronándolo con su blanco caserío como si fuera una corona de muerto" [55:95].

Luvina is the home of sadness and despair, a place where the dead "live" and the living are "dead," and where the few withered human beings who remain there refuse to flee and leave behind their dead. "Pero si nosotros nos vamos," they say, "¿quien se llevará a nuestros muertos? Ellos viven aquí y no podemos dejarlos solos" [55:103]. And besides, to the outside world, these people are already dead. "No saben si existen," the narrator explains, and the only time their existence is

recognized is when the government sends someone to Luvina to fetch
and kill one of its residents who has done something wrong.

Therefore, surrounded on all sides and from within by death, they
sit and wait, "sentados en sus puertas, con los brazos caídos. . . .Sólos,
en aquella soledad de Luvina" [55:102]. "Nadie lleva la cuenta de las
horas ni a nadie le preocupa cómo van amontonándose los años. Los
días comienzan y se acaban. Luego viene la noche. Solamente el día
y la noche hasta el día de la muerte, que para ellos es una esperanza"
[55:101].

The comparison is often drawn between Luvina and Comala, the
setting of Rulfo's novel Pedro Páramo. It seems certain that in creating
Luvina Rulfo was paving the way for the creation of Comala, a village
of real ghosts. As Hugo Rodríquez Alcala points out, " . . .si Comala
es un pueblo de muertos, de fantasmas, Luvina es un pueblo de vivos
que apenas viven. . . .Comala existe fuera del tiempo o, mejor en un
tiempo eternizado. Luvina tambien existe fuera del tiempo. Allí 'todo
se queda quieto, sin tiempo, como si se viviera en la eternidad,' . . .
Si en Comala hay sólo fantasmas, los hombres y mujeres de Luvina
parecen fantasmas. El narrador nos cuenta: 'Vi a todas las mujeres de
Luvina con su cántaro al hombro, con el rebozo colgado de su cabeza y
sus figuras negras sobre el negro fondo de la noche' "[56:48-49].

In "Luvina", time is of little significance. As Ramón Xirau tells
us, "Luvina se acerca, más que ningún otro, a la negación total del
tiempo" [57:4]. Or as James Irby says, "Todo parece estar suspendido
en el tiempo, casi muerto, sólo esperando el lento desmoronar de las
cosas que acabará al fin con la existencia. Como en todos los relatos del
Rulfo, el tiempo—dimensión con la cual se mide la acción humana—ha
perdido su significado. No hay pasado ni futuro, sólo hay un presente
eternamente agonizante. Lo explica el narrador anónimo: 'Me parece
que usted me preguntó cuántos años estuve en Luvina, ¿verdad? . . .La
verdad es que no lo sé. Perdí la noción del tiempo desde que las fiebres
me lo enrevesaron; pero debió haber sido una eternidad. . . .Y es que allá
el tiempo es muy largo. Nadie lleva la cuenta de las horas ni a nadie le
preocupa cómo van amontonándose los años . . .' "[58: 140-41]. Thus,
there appears to be little difference between the timeless world depicted
in these stories and the dead world depicted in Pedro Páramo.

As in other stories of the collection, such as "Macario" and "Es
que somos muy pobres," there is no actual human death depicted in

"Luvina." And yet, setting and atmosphere clearly insinuate the presence of death. "Buen numero de los cuentos de *El llano en llamas* no puede eludir la presencia de la muerte, y 'Luvina' . . .va a mostrar una nueva manera de tratarla por las insinuaciones propias del ambiente y del aire particular de sus hombres subsumidos en él. El sobrecogimiento que invade el ánimo en una relectura de 'Luvina' es por la presencia de la muerte" [59:13].

The same atmosphere present in "Luvina" is present throughout the collection. For as Emmanuel Carballo points out, "Rulfo es un cuentista monocorde que expresa un mundo angosto en el que todos los lugares—los scenarios—son mas o menos iguales" [60]. His is a world "desprovisto de sentido y orden, donde las cosas suceden fatalmente, porque sí, escapando a cualquier explicación lógica o racional; un mundo hostil en el que está desterrado, impotente, el hombre" [58:135], a world "dedicated to the cult of death" [51:266].

Setting, though, is often primarily a reflection of the psyche of the characters in a given literary work, as several outstanding literary theorists have pointed out. For example, Wellek and Warren state: "Setting is environment, and environments . . . may be viewed as metonymic, or metaphoric, expressions of character. A man's house is an extension of himself. Describe it and you have described him . . . Setting may be the expression of a human will. It may, if it is a natural setting, be a projection of the will. Says the self-analyst Amiel, 'A landscape is a state of mind.' Between man and nature there are obvious correlatives" [61:221].

The cult of death is a social phenomenon, a psychological phenomenon, and it is best reflected in people and their actions. Let us, then, turn to the discussion of a story in which characterization serves as the outstanding vehicle of expression of the phenomenon: "La Cuesta de las Comadres."

The story is essentially an account, in the first person, of the killing of Remigio Torrico whom the narrator, an old friend of the Torricos, stabbed through the navel and heart with a harness needle. It is an emotionless, though graphic, account of an act which we cannot help but feel should arouse more emotion. But it is precisely the lack of emotion displayed herein which makes this story such an excellent portrayal of the typical Rulfian hero. In the persons of the narrator and the other characters to whom he introduces us, we find embodied most of the attitudes so often associated with the cult of death and so often reflected in all of Rulfo's works—stoic resignation, fatalism, insouciant violence. The narrator accepts impassively the Torricos' murder of the mule driver, and he displays no emotion in his description of the deaths of the Torricos, one at his own hands. And perhaps even more significantly, he does nothing to avert the situation which brings about the death of Remigio, when a simple explanation of the facts as he knew them might have done just that. Rulfo's characters in this story, as in so many others, are conspicuously lacking in free will, and their stoic acceptance of their situation reflects itself not only in their attitude toward life, but in their attitude toward death. The ultra-passive attitude which the narrator and the other characters of "La Cuesta de las Comadres" assume in the face of acts of violence and their failure to act to prevent them reflect the nonchalance of a people "for whom death is always close and life has little value" [51:260).

Speaking of the Rulfian hero in general. Raul Chavarri tells us, "Los héroes de Rulfo son siempre héroes pasivos . . .los héroes menos heroicos que pueden encontrarse. No hay en ellos la serena actitud de revelarse [sic] contra la fortuna, no se 'toman las armas contra un piélago de calamidades.' sino que simplemente se sufre esto que los ocurre" [62:175]. Thus, the people of the hill of the comadres do not resist the tyranny of the Torricos, two men against fifty-eight; they simply leave their lands never to return. "Se iban callados la boca. sin decir nada ni pelearse con nadie. Es seguro que les sobraban ganas de pelearse con los Torricos para desquitarse de todo el mal que les habían hecho; pero no tuvieron ánimos. Seguro eso pasó. La cosa es que todavía después de que murieron los Torricos nadie volvió más por aquí. Yo estuve esperando. Pero nadie regresó" [75:22].

As Diane Hill points out, the "matter-of-fact" tone that his characters display "nos dice mucho sobre la perspectiva de Juan Rulfo; no sólo su perspectiva literaria, sino también su actitud hacia el hombre individual. El hombre no es mas que otro elemento del mundo. No tiene más importancia ni más significado que los demás componentes de la realidad. . . .Este efecto se logra mediante una actitud ultrarealista, en la que la descripción de una muerte o la de un árbol son iquales en su falta de sentimiento. El árbol y la muerte participant, ambos, de una sola realidad; de modo que ni el uno ni la otra tiene mas importancia dentro del esquema general de esa realidad. EI mundo existe por sí mismo, como entidad objetiva, y la presencia o falta de un árbol más o un hombre más no lo altera ni lo afecta profundamente" [63:338]. The narrator tells us that when he gave the dead mule driver one last kick, "sonó iqual que si se la hubiera dado a un tronco seco" [75:25]. And somehow we feel that the comparison is well drawn.

Exterior character description is conspicuously lacking in all of Rulfo's stories. We know, for example, that Remigio Torrico had only one eye, "black and half-closed," but, aside from that, we know nothing of the physiognomy of the characters in "La Cuesta de las Comadres." And, yet, with characteristic verbal economy, Rulfo provides us with such a vivid impression of the attitudes and ways of life of his characters that we see them better than if they had been described to us in detail. It is as if we view his characters from the inside out, rather than from the outside in. And the outstanding element of their personalities viewed from this perspective is their attitude toward life and death.

If we bear in mind the earlier discussion of the historical bases of the cult of death, we will note more than a small remnant of indigenous philosophy in the attitudes of Rulfo's characters, especially here in "La Cuesta de las Comadres"—the lack of concern for the individual, the acceptance of death as a part of the natural order of existence with no apparent concern for its redeeming quality or for the Christian concept of repentance and salvation. And, yet, the phenomenon displayed herein is far more than a simple holdover of ancient indigenous attitudes. It is the product of years of fusion and social development. It is that modern phenomenon described earlier and so effectively by Octavio Paz, a phenomenon based upon years of tradition and, yet, in itself unique.

Many have accused Rulfo of *tremendista* techniques, his stories being steeped in blood, violence, and death. But as José de la Colina points out, "su creación bebe en una fuente inexhausta de la tradición mexicana, . . . [donde] se encuentra ese mismo tono directo, sencillo, cortado, para hablar de la crueldad como de una cosa cotidiana y común, y de la muerte que Ie puede suceder a cualquiera, en cualquier momento. EI mexicano se siente sumergido en un mundo indiferente y cruel, en el que la vida, . . . 'no vale nada' [64:136].

And, finally, we should allude to one factor common to the lives of all of the characters in *El llano en llamas*, the state of solitude in which they all live. Octavio Paz relates the solitude of the Mexican to his fascination for death and to his propensity toward seemingly senseless acts of violence. Violence, as he sees it, is a means by which the Mexican escapes the solitude of his everyday life, and it is often his only means of communicating with his fellow man, or, more accurately, it is a natural result of his inability to do so. Thus, instead of communicating the facts of his brother's death to Remigio Torrico, the narrator of the story kills him. The fascination that death exerts over the Mexican, Paz tells us, is also perhaps the result of his hermit-like solitude and of the fury with which he breaks out of it [45:39-54].

"La Cuesta de las Comadres" well illustrates Rulfo's use of characterization as a vehicle of expression of the Mexican cult of death. But it is only representative of a number of stories which might have been cited. As Claude Couffon points out, "En la mayoría de los personajes de Rulfo, la muerte está escondida, dispuesta a brincar o brincando. Ella es la consecuencia lógica de esta violencia que atormenta todas las mentes, una violencia inútil por cierto, pero para estos seres toscos, sin educación, parece la única manera de exorcizar la realidad: el hambre, el aislamiento, la falta de trabajo, la inclemencia de la naturaleza" [65:47]. For Rulfo's characters and, as has been noted previously, for many Mexicans, violence and death are "the ultimate means to salvage prestige."

George D. Schade well sums up the relationship of characterization and the cult of death in *El llano en llamas*: "Rulfo peels many of his characters down to the core, but some of them, like the landscape, frequently clouded over and hazy, remain blurred, imprecise, and taciturn figures. They are never seen in full face, but always in a silhouette. like the lugubrious, black-garbed crones of 'Luvina.' The one thing standing forth clear and ubiquitous is death-overpowering life-which seems to hold scant value in this world" [66:x].

In *El llano en llamas*, character and setting combine to create a picture of a world which is static, timeless, and always hostile toward man, who has somehow learned to become either indifferent or resigned to it. It is a world in which action of any sort seems futile, for all of life in the world of *El llano en llamas* is predetermined and any action on the part of any character to try to alter or improve his world is destined to failure. The only "action" in these stories consists of various senseless and fruitless acts of violence, acts which are born rather from a feeling of indifference toward life and death than from any sense of purpose, other than revenge.

In a world in which living is often a static, meaningless experience, dying is often the only real form of action. As Alfonso León de Garay states, "morir es siempre una forma disponible de actuar, no de esperar" [67:59]. But even these acts are usually nothing more than senseless manifestations of repressed hostilities due to years of suffering and inertia. Thus, James Irby tells us of *El llano en llamas*, "No hay acción; los personajes no hacen nada. Hasta las muertes que estos infligen cruelmente a sus semejantes parecen ser actos ajenos a su voluntad y ellos sólo los vehículos obedientes de una ira que desciende como un rayo del cielo. He aquí, pues, las dos constantes que rigen el vivir y el morir en el mundo de Rulfo: pasividad ensimismada y violencia inexplicable" [58:149].

Action in the short stories of Juan Rulfo, then, if it exists, invariably takes the form of violence and death and thereby serves as another vehicle of expression of the Mexican cult of death. Let us again look at a story to illustrate this point.

"El llano en llamas," the story that gives the collection its name, is the longest story therein and also the one in which we find the most action in the usual sense of the word. It is a story of the Mexican Revolution, but the Revolution here has lost the epic quality displayed in many of the great works it inspired. All that remains in Rulfo's story is the senseless death and destruction it engendered. As El Pichón, narrator of the story, and his comrades set out again to join Pedro Zamora after a brief defeat-inspired peace, he tells us, "Seguimos caminando de frente, encandilados por la luminaria de San Buenaventura, como si algo nos dijera que nuestro trabajo era estar allí, para acabar con lo que quedara"[55:73]. Here is a case of violence inspiring violence with no further purpose. "Era más fácil caer sobre los ranchos en lugar de estar emboscando a las tropas del gobierno" [55:76].

Then later we witness the cruel *juego del toro* in which Pedro Zamora playing the bull and armed with his razor-sharp sword playfully executes his prisoners. There is a sense of cold-blooded indifference to human suffering in the scene that especially distinguishes it. There is also the train wreck in which so many soldiers and their women die, the consequences of which had not been foreseen by Zamora's men and fill them with fear. "No sabíamos bien a bien lo que iba a suceder" [55:80], Pichón tells us, and we realize that throughout the story there is a complete lack of concern for human life and that the action displayed therein is blind and meaningless. Only death seems to have any real control over life. "En todos los lugares triunfa la muerte, la cruel muerte mexicana que encuentra su representación simbólica en el cadaver del 'Chihuila' atejonado detrás de un madroño, con la cobija envuelta alrededor del pescuezo, y que 'parecía estar riéndose de nosotros, con sus dientes pelones, colorados de sangre' "[65].

And, finally, the manner in which El Pichón relates the most atrocious acts, as if they were the most normal, commonplace events, attests more than any other aspect of the story to the existence of a cult of death.

But there is another interesting aspect of the work. I have alluded earlier to the Mexican's strikingly fatalistic and stoic nature as a much noted psychological manifestation of the cult of death. In most of Rulfo's works, feelings of despair, hopelessness, and pessimism emanate from this fatalism and stoicism: this explains in part their lack of conclusions and their often circular quality.

"El llano en llamas" is the only story in the collection in which the typical Rulfian pessimism seems to have been tempered significantly. It is the only story in which there is a conclusion in the strict sense of the term. El Pichón is redeemed from his life of banditry and starts out upon a new life with the woman who has waited for him during his years in jail and with their son who, although he shares his father's name and a certain meanness of look, "no es ningún bandido ni ningún asesino. El es gente buena"[55:84]. "El llano en llamas," then, reminds us that the cult of death, if viewed from a national rather than a Rulfian perspective, does not by its very nature imply a completely negative outlook toward life.

The three stories discussed above well illustrate Juan Rulfo's use of setting, characterization, and action as vehicles of expression of the Mexican cult of death in the stories of *El llano en llamas*. My choice of stories to illustrate the use of each of these elements has been more or less arbitrary; as in most of the stories of the collection, the cult of death stands out as the underlying leit motif. As George Schade tells us, "The elements of the harsh physical environment combine with the Mexican Indian's fatalism to forge almost a symbiosis of man and landscape. The parched, dry plain is overwhelming. The Indian accepts life as it is there, and his acts are almost inevitable . . . . Impotence and despair reign, and death rattles in the scorching air, the howling wind, the throttling dust of the plain" [66:xiv].

It is true that Rulfo expresses only certain elements of the cult of death in Mexico. We see little of the more positive manifestations of the phenomenon—the friendly humor with which death is often treated, the gaiety surrounding certain festivals and attractions in which death is the main object of festivity, the beauty of death-inspired art, etc. Rulfo presents to us only its more somber elements—psychological elements such as resignation, stoicism, fatalism, pessimism, and physical elements such as violence and death by violence. But Rulfo's style, limited as it may be, faithfully reflects the world in which his stories are set, the world of the Jaliscan campesino. And his stories, in general, reflect faithfully a phenomenon which dates back to the first indigenous myth of creation. As Arturo Torres-Rioseco points out in reference to Rulfo's novel *Pedro Páramo*, "The cult of death occupies a luminous spot in Mexican mythology, and in modern times death is considered merely the inverse of life. In Mexican painting, from Posada to Orozco and Montenegro, the skeleton is an omnipresent figure. Entire books have been written on the skull in Mexican art. Such vital artists as Diego Rivera and Alfaro Siqueiros maintain constant contact with death. It should not surprise us then that an author like Juan Rulfo should choose a village of corpses as a setting for his novel" [68:83]. Neither should it surprise us that Rulfo chose a village like Luvina for the setting of one of his short stories or that the cult of death occupies a luminous spot in each of the stories of *El llano en llamas*.

Rulfo is, as Reinaldo Arenas comments, "el escritor más admirado y el autor mexicano que mayor prestigio ha adquirido en la literatura occidental" [69:113-28]. Certainly his fame is due in part to the style and artistry of expression displayed in his works. But in greater part I feel that his popularity is due to the fact that Rulfo's stories reflect a national phenomenon which is in essence a key to the understanding of the Mexican soul; the reader not only sees but feels that phenomenon as Rulfo causes him to enter the soul of his characters and to view the world from their perspective and to become, for a short while at least, a part of that world. No other writer better suits our discussion of the manifestations of the cult of death in the contemporary Mexican short story, for Rulfo is certainly the outstanding exponent of that phenomenon in literature.

But the cult of death is a nationally felt and expressed phenomenon and is by no means limited to the works of one author. Let us turn to a discussion of manifestations of the cult of death in the short stories of several other outstanding figures of Mexican literature.

It has been noted that all of Rulfo's works are set in Jalisco, the state in which he was born and raised. For this reason, critics have sometimes accused him of displaying only a limited, regional view of Mexican life. José Revueltas was born in the city of Durango and was raised and educated in Mexico City; yet, one notices several striking similarities between his works and Rulfo's, especially in regard to the cult of death. Examination of some of Revueltas' short stories will help to establish that the cult of death is by no means a regional phenomenon and that it manifests itself in the short stories of writers from all regions of Mexico.

Revueltas is best known as a novelist. His second novel, *El luto humano* (1943), won the Premio Nacional de Literatura and made its author an internationally acclaimed literary figure. His next work, published in 1944, was a collection of short stories entitled *Dios en la tierra*, and this too received considerable critical acclaim. Since then short stories by José Revueltas have been included in the best anthologies and collections of the Mexican short story and appear consistently in leading Mexican journals. In 1960 Revueltas published another collection of eight short stories, similar in thematic content to *Dios en la tierra*, entitled *Dormir en tierra*. It is with the manifestations of the cult of death in a number of the stories from this collection that I shall concern myself.

Clara Passafari de Gutiérrez tells us that *Dormir en tierra* "aborda el tema raigal de la muerte y su formidable sentido y gravitación sobre el destino de los hombres" [70:161]. Death is certainly a central theme in most of the short stories of *Dormir en tierra*, but outstanding among these as a vehicle of expression of the cult of death is the second story of the collection, "La frontera increíble."

In this story Revueltas examines the transitional state between life and death, "el sitio preciso de la transición reveladora y demoníaca entre la vida y la muerte" [71:44]. The reader of this story views death from two perspectives, that of the living, in this case the family of the dying man and the priest who administers the last rites, and that of the dying man himself, and he sees that the two perspectives are irreconcilable—that there comes a point after which communication is impossible between the living and the dying, though the dying person be still technically alive. Thus, the family's concept of their loved one's death is considerably different from that of the dying man himself. "Nada alteraba el silencio recogido y humilde de la habitación. Los párpados quietos del agonizante hacían pensar que su muerte iba a ser tranquila, sin sufrimiento, no como esas muertes angustiosas en que la casa se llena de terror y hay un deseo tremendo de que todo ocurra de una vez, sin transiciones, para que cese el espectáculo intolerable del moribundo que gime o grita como una encarnación del espanto" [71:39]. To those who observed his death, it seemed a peaceful one; but revealed from within the subconscious of the dying man, it is seen to be quite another thing.

> Testimonio, cuerpo mío, duéleme, que eres mi último sufrimiento antes de que me entregue al sufrimiento puro, al que no tiene principio ni fin, ni mezcla de alegría ni de esperanza.   [71:42]

> El cuerpo del agonizante, en el paroxismo del dolor, empezó a asirse a él. al agonizante, a abrazarlo con rabia, con una angustia no experimentada jamás. El moribundo amaba y despreciaba esta lucha, esta ruptura alta, horrible y oscuramente bella.   [71:44]

The dying man is able to perceive the living, but he is in a different world now, totally alone, and he can no longer communicate with them. As he explains it, " . . .como todos los hombres aún no tocados por Ia luz de la muerte, aquellos no tenían entre sí otro medio de comunicación que la palabra. Su territorio era la palabra. Su patria era la palabra. Su habitación era la palabra. Pero nada más. ¿Cómo comunicarles, entonces, la verdad de la muerte, si él poseía ahora un lenguaje extraño y antiguo, no comprensible para nadie sobre la tierra? . . . el impenetrable idioma de la muerte" [71:42-43]. Thus, the last paragraph of the work states, "En medio de su dolor, todos experimentaron una cierta tranquilidad melancólica, pues la muerte, como lo imaginaran, había sido suave, dulce, sin sufrimiento alguno" [71:45].

In "La frontera increíble," one is able to observe the feelings of guilt, remorse, and fear of the living and their misinterpretation and misunderstanding of the physical and emotional state of the dying man; one is also able to perceive the thoughts and reactions of the dying man as he enters that *frontera increíble* which separates him forever from the living who surround him. Thus, the story, a most interesting and original study of the act of dying, is a fine manifestation of the cult of death in the contemporary Mexican short story.

"Lo que solo uno escucha" expresses many of the same themes as "La frontera increíble," loneliness, lack of communication, and death. It is a beautiful story of the swan song of a smalltime Mexican violinist, Rafael, who finds himself suddenly playing as he has never played before. "Los trémolos, patéticos y graves, vibraban en el espacio con limpidez y diafanidad sin ejemplo, los acordes se sucedían en las más dichosas y transparentes combinaciones, los arpegios eran ágiles y llenos de juventud. Todo lo mejor de la tierra se daba cita en aquella música; las más bellas y fecundas ideas elevábanse del espíritu y el violín era como un instrumento mágico destinado a consumar las más altas comuniones" [71:107].

Rafael's happiness is profound; yet, an inborn fatalism and stoicism prevent him from revealing his feeling to anyone, and his happiness reveals itself merely as "un aire estúpido," a look which leads his family to ask him if he is sick. In the fatalistic world in which Rafael and his family live, happiness is "un pecado que no se puede confesar," and any revelation of such feelings only causes feelings of alarm on the part of those to whom they are revealed.

> "¿Estas enfermo?" preguntaron a coro y con ansiedad los niños. Rafael no respondió sino con su sonrisa lastimera y lejana.
> "No les diré una palabra. Lo que me ocurre es como un pecado que no se puede confesar." Y al decirse esto, Rafael sintió un tremendo impulso de ponerse en pie y dar a su mujer un beso en la frente, pero lo detuvo la idea de que aquello le causaría alarma.   [71:106]

As Edmundo Valadés points out, "el hombre revueltiano está destinado a lo peor" [72:22]. While Rafael is joyously thinking to himself of the beautiful change that will now take place in his life, his wife is seeing in her husband's look the undeniable omen of death. "Ahora cambiará todo," Rafael says to himself. "Será todo distinto. Todo cambiará" [71:104]. But his wife is thinking "ese brillo humilde en los ojos y esa dulzura torpe en los labios . . .es un anuncio de la muerte. No puede ser sino la muerte. ¿Pero como decírselo? ¿Como darle consuelo? ¿Como prepararlo para el pavoroso instante?" [71:106].

Rafael is now like the protagonist of "La frontera increíble," a dying man, though he himself does not know it; and, therefore, communication between him and his wife is no longer possible.

"Toda comunicación profunda entre sus dos ánimas se había roto ya" [71:106]. Thus his wife says one thing and means another, and Rafael's feeble attempt to express his feelings is interpreted merely as a sign of drunkenness. Revueltas' characters, like Rulfo's, are completely lacking in free will. Therefore, Rafael, with no signs of protest, allows himself to be led to his bed where he dies. In a fatalistic world, it seems, happiness and death invariably go hand in hand.

"Los hombres en el pantano" is a different type of story. It is the story of a patrol of Mexican-American soldiers in World War II, trapped in a swamp somewhere in the Pacific, playing a life-or-death game of hide-and-seek with a patrol of Japanese. The first paragraph of the story explains essentially all of the rest. "La cuestion era escuchar algo vivo, y todos esperaban que este anhelado acontecimiento se produjera una vez más, de cualquier modo y como fuese, después de las dos ocasiones, ya tan lejanas al parecer, en que había ocurrido y en que esto los hizo respirar con un alivio cínico, puro y ruin, ahí metidos como estaban, con el agua cenagosa hasta el pecho" [71:49].

In the static world depicted in this story, death, the death of another, serves as a type of proof of life for those who remain. "Se trataba únicamente de oírse, de oírse nada más, y no importaba que el grito representara una baja japonesa o norteamericana, sino que todos supieran, mediante ese grito, mediante esa muerte, que cada uno de ellos no estaba solo ni muerto sobre la superficie de la tierra" [71:50]. Yet movement and sound, life as it were, signify death. " . . . algún imprudente o loco se había movido, . . .produciendo un rumor asombrosamente claro, preciso, increíble ahí en el pantano donde aquello significaba la muerte. . . .los hechos no eran sino testimonies, un modo de vivir, un modo de atestiguarse cada uno a si mismo con la muerte" [71:50-51].

The static world described in the following quotation—a world in which life is a living death and death and violence are the only manifestations of life—displays an unmistakable resemblance to the static world described in the short stories of Juan Rulfo. " . . .ya no eran seres reales, . . .habían dejado de ser hombres y no podían encontrar ninguna otra manifestación de vida sino en la muerte: . . .lo único humano y viviente que les quedaba en la existencia era el aullido de los que morían, . . .la única acción viva que les estaba permitida, era la acción de matar" [71:55].

In the discussion of manifestations of the cult of death in the short stories of Juan Rulfo, several elements are consistently referred to by critics as characteristically "Rulfian"—elements such as fatalism, stoic resignation, lack of free will, and solitude—elements in Mexican literature associated with the cult of death and evident in the setting, characterization, and action of the short stories of *El llano en llamas*. The following comments are by two outstanding critics of José Revueltas' works, but they might well have been said of the works of Juan Rulfo; they attest to the fact that Revueltas, too, in a manner similar to Rulfo's, manifests in his short stories the Mexican cult of death. James Irby, for example, observes that the works of José Revueltas are characterized by "un materialismo estático y muerto y un fatalismo atroz que anulan acción y movimiento y crean personajes unilaterales, sin desarrollo interno, meras figuras." And he tells us that "en la obra de Revueltas se crea a menudo un ambiente denso y sofocante, misterioso y oscuro, un ambiente que las más de las veces evoca la miseria, el pathos, el terror y la soledad" [58:113]. Alí Chumacero notes that Revueltas' characters emerge from "una región demasiado hecha de una pieza, entera y uniforme, como descendida de una voluntad ajena, separada del hombre mismo. Así la voluntad humana resulta nacida de una fuerza muy otra que la conciencia. No obedece a propio impulso ni actúa por propia convicción" [73:5].

When speaking of the short stories of *Dios en la tierra* and Revueltas' works in general. James Irby refers to certain outstanding themes—misery, desperation, sex, infirmity, hatred, terror, and death [58:122]. These same themes persist in the stories of *Dormir en tierra*, with one of the outstanding themes being that of death. Death is the central theme of the three stories discussed herein, and it is present in each of the remaining stories of the collection; for example, life as a living death and early suicide are depicted in "La hermana enemiga," the story of a young girl victimized by a step-sister who makes her ashamed of her sex and who finally drives her to commit suicide, a suicide which is almost anticlimactic in view of the life she had been leading. "Agotada y temblorosa se puso en pie y caminó hasta el centro de la habitación, donde, quieta y muda, quiso pensar en la muerte con toda su alma, pero le fue imposible pues era como si ya hubíese muerto irremediablemente desde antes" [71:82].

In "El lenguaje de nadie," an ignorant Indian buries his old mistress alive, thinking her dead of typhus, and when she beats upon the coffin in an attempt to free herself, he assumes that it is her spirit which is trying to frighten him and he buries her nonetheless. His act is judged a product of ignorance by the court before which he appears, but in consequence he is forced to sign over the piece of land which has been left to him in the old woman's will.

Each of these stories, as well as the others of the collection, attests to the fact that manifestations of the Mexican cult of death do exist in, and are an outstanding feature of, the short stories of José Revueltas.

To further illustrate the contention that the cult of death is by no means a purely regional phenomenon and that it manifests itself in the short stories of writers from various regions of Mexico, we move south to the state of Chiapas and to a discussion of the short stories of Rosario Castellanos.

Rosario Castellanos, like José Revueltas, is best known as a novelist. Her novels *Balúm Canán* (1957) and *Oficio de tinieblas* (1962) have been translated into several major world tongues. Her poetry, too, has received considerable attention. Of her short stories, though, little has been written in the way of critical material, although they are invariably included in the outstanding collections of the genre in Mexico and appear often in leading Mexican journals. *Ciudad Real*, published in 1960, is a collection of ten stories and is described on the back cover of the book as being "un retrato fiel de esta ciudad chiapaneca, más fiel aún por no ser una casual imagen fotográfica, sino la aguda percepción del sitio expresada con hábiles recursos artísticos; la autora colaboró con los antropólogos y los médicos que luchan por resolver los problemas de la region, y fruto de sus experiencias es este tomo en que recrea el mundo de los indígenas, de los ladinos" [74].

Although manifestations of the cult of death appear in only three or four stories of this collection, those that do appear provide a faithful image of the phenomenon as it exists in that region of southern Mexico. The second story of *Ciudad Real*, entitled "La tregua," particularly well suits our discussion. The cult of death depicted in this story is that of pre-Conquest Mexico, untainted by Christian teachings.

When a stranger, a *caxlán*, or "white man," arrives in Mukenjá—ostensibly to solicit help from the residents, as he is obviously sick but unable to communicate his purpose to them since he speaks a different language—he is immediately assumed by the Indian woman Rominka to be the disguised wandering spirit of "*el pukuj*, dueño de los montes, dueño de todas las cosas," the bringer of madness, the killer of children. Rominka, after begging for her life, runs to her hut where she encloses herself with all of her children except one whom she sends for the men. The men, in their turn, also assume that the stranger must be a harbinger of death, in the form either of a revenue agent or of the dreaded god; for both, to the Indians of Mukenjá, forced by their poverty into illegally producing and distributing aguardiente, signify death. They think back to when the Secretario Municipal, Rodolfo López, and his men, inconvenienced by their long search for the source of the bootleg aguardiente which had been affecting legal sales, apprehend the Indians responsible for its production and burn them in their huts. ". . .cuando la paja comenzó a arder y las paredes crujieron y quienes estaban adentro quisieron huir, Rodolfo López los obligó a regresar a culatazos. Y respiró, con el ansia del que ha estado a punto de asfixiarse, el humo de la carne achicarrada" [74:33].

But an innate fatalism and stoic resignation forbid the men any thoughts of flight. "Cualquiera de las dos posibilidades era ineluctable y tratar de evadirla o de aplazarla con un intento de fuga era un esfuerzo malgastado. Los varones de Mukenjá afrontaron la situación sin pensar siquiera en sus instrumentos de labranza como en armas defensivas. Inermes, fueron de regreso al caserío" [74:34].

So the men return to their village to face whatever awaits them there. The sight of the weakened stranger, unable to stand, and Rominka's repetition of the word "pukuj" excites in them a mad thirst for revenge over this power who brings sickness, famine, and death to their village.

> Pukuj. Por la mala influencia de éste que yacía aquí, a sus pies, las cosechas no eran nunca suficientes, los brujos comían a los rebaños, las enfermedades no los perdonaban. En vano los indios habían intentado congraciarse con su potencia oscura por medio de ofrendas y sacrificios. El pukuj continuaba escogiendo sus víctimas. Y ahora, empujado por quién sabe que necesidad, por quién sabe que codicia, había abandonado su madriguera y, disfrazado de ladino, andaba las serranías, atajaba a los caminantes. . . .Los varones requirieron lo que hallaron más a mano para el ataque: garrotes, piedras, machetes. Una mujer, con un incensario humeante, dió varias vueltas alrededor del caído, trazando un círculo mágico que ya no podría trasponer. Entonces la furia se desencadenó. Garrote que golpea, piedra que machaca el cráneo, machete que cercena los miembros. Las mujeres gritaban, detrás de la pared de los jacales, enardeciendo a los varones para que consumaran su obra criminal. [74:35]

But the truce brought about by the blood of "el pukuj" is of short duration, and soon the Indians turn again to thoughts of blood sacrifice. " . . .la tregua no fue duradera. Nuevos espíritus malignos infestaron el aire. Y las cosechas de Mukenjá fueron ese año tan escasas como antes. Los brujos, comedores de bestias, comedores de hombres, exigían su alimento. Las enfermedades también los diezmaban. Era preciso volver a matar" [74:36].

In this story of a small Chiapan Indian village, we see reflected and perpetuated the attitudes toward life and death of the pre-Conquest Mexican, fatalism, stoic resignation, and the belief in blood sacrifice as a requisite for the prolongation of life. The cult of death manifested herein is little different from that of pre-Conquest, Aztec Mexico.

In the other stories of *Ciudad Real*, death is a less prominent theme, but in several of these a sense of indifference toward death, especially on the part of the Indian population, is evident. When Mariano Sántiz Nich's eleven-year-old son dies in "Arthur Smith salva su alma," "su indiferencia exasperó a Arthur" [74:173]. The only thing that their new religion seems to have brought to these Indians is a more concrete hope for the alleviation of their suffering after death. "Mi hijo mayor está en el cielo. Allá no hay hambre, no hay frío, no hay palo. Allá está contento," says Mariano, but this hope does little to attenuate his indifference toward life and toward the physical aspect of death.

In "La rueda del hambriento," the nurse, Alicia, seems to be the only person who feels any concern for the life and death of a new-born Indian child. "El pukuj se está comiendo a mi hijo," says the child's father, and neither he nor the child's grandfather make any attempt to go and get the money which would save the child's life. Nor is the doctor willing to volunteer sustenance for the child, because he believes, and rightly so perhaps, that in that way he will never gain the Indians' respect and esteem.

And, finally, in "Cuarta vigilia," "la niña Nides" is completely indifferent when she murders an innocent Indian in order to insure the secrecy of the hiding place of her money which she never spends.

The theme of death is not as omnipresent in the stories of Rosario Castellanos as it is in those of Juan Rulfo and José Revueltas, but it is present in isolated stories. "La tregua," for example, displays the cult of death as it appears today in many of the isolated Indian villages of Mexico, where attitudes toward life and death are still a direct holdover from those of their inhabitants' most remote ancestors.

Sharing with Juan Rulfo the title of most prestigious Mexican writer is Carlos Fuentes, an internationally renowned and prolific novelist, short-story writer, and critic. Rulfo himself, when asked in one of his rare interviews, "¿Qué autores mexicanos destacaría usted?" replied with customary modesty, "A Carlos Fuentes. El es la base de toda literatura joven actual de Mexico. Todos quieren ser como él. Pero no es fácil, ya que Fuentes, cuando comenzó a escribir, poseía una cultura muy amplia" [75:3]. In Miguel Donoso Pareja's opinion. "Carlos Fuentes continúa siendo en Mexico el Sumo sacerdote de la literatura juvenile, refiriéndonos a la prosa naturalmente. . . .ha sabido mantenerse a la cabeza de los narradores mexicanos jóvenes" [76:12].

Fuentes' fame, like that of José Revueltas and Rosario Castellanos, rests most heavily upon his novels. These have been translated and acclaimed the world over. But Fuentes' first work, published in 1954, was not a novel but a collection of six short stories entitled *Los días enmascarados*. Ten years later he published another volume of seven short stories, *Cantar de ciegos*, and, of course, he has written innumerable stories for publication in leading national and international journals and anthologies since that time.

Of Fuentes' second volume of short stories, *Cantar de ciegos,* Richard Reeves states that "these pieces demonstrate a significant departure from those in *Los días enmascarados* in their lack of thesis and emphasis on entertainment. Several characters are typical mid-twentieth-century types who are universal in their interests rather than national or Mexican" [77:610]. Though Rubén Salazar Mallén points out that "en todos los cuentos está presente un agudo pesimismo, un notorio desprecio hacia el ser humano y un evidente desencanto de la vida" [78:38].

Despite the presence of such elements–elements often associated with the cult of death—the universal, cosmopolitan quality of these stories renders them less applicable to the discussion of our topic than those of Fuentes' first volume, *Los días enmascarados.* [5] My discussion of manifestations of the cult of death in the short stories of Carlos Fuentes will, therefore, focus on two stories from that work. This first volume is also more significant as it marks the direction of much of Fuentes' later work.

The six stories of *Los días enmascarados,* with the exception of the second, "En defensa de la Trigolibia," which is of a purely political nature, are a combination of realism and the purest fantasy. The first of these, entitled "Chac Mool." is considered by the author and by most critics to be the best of the collection. The story is retrospective; it begins at the end, and, little by little, it works backward to reveal the central incident upon which it is built.

Its beginning strictly adheres to logic. "Hace poco tiempo, Filiberto murió ahogado en Acapulco" [80:55]. And there appears to be a logical explanation. "Claro sabíamos que en su juventud había nadado bien,

---

5   The title of this work, *Los días enmascarados,* alludes to the last five days of the Aztec year, the "nemontani," "cinco días sin nombre, días vacíos durante los cuales se suspendía toda actividad—frágil puente entre el fin de un año y el comienzo de otro" (79:iv). It also brings to mind Chapter II, "Máscaras mexicanas," of Octavio Paz's *El laberinto de la soledad* [35], by which Fuentes is said to have been influenced, especially in the writing of this volume.

pero ahora a los cuarenta, y tan desmejorado como se le veía, ¡intentar salvar, ya medianoche, un trecho tan largo'" [80:55]. It is not until halfway through the story, as the narrator proceeds with his reading of Filiberto's diary, that the fantastic element is introduced into the narrative, to the point where, by the end of the story, it has completely overshadowed the realism of the first portion of the work.

Filiberto. a collector of pre-Columbian artifacts, purchases a statue of Chac Mool, the Aztec god of rain, in a Mexico City flea market, the Lagunilla, and upon returning home places the statue in his basement. Shortly afterward, the basement mysteriously floods, returning the Chac Mool to its legendary natural element and giving to the statue a slimy, fleshy appearance which no efforts on Filiberto's part are able to erase. Still there appears to be a logical explanation; "este mercador de la Lagunilla me ha timado. Su escultura precolombina es puro yeso, y la humedad acabará por arruinarla" [80:61]. But from this point of the narrative on, reality fades and fantasy takes over as Chac Mool takes on a living form, appears to Filiberto, and gains complete control over him. In a last effort to escape his captor, Filiberto flees to Acapulco, where he is drowned.

Even to the last page of the story, one is able to apply a logical explanation to the events recounted in Filiberto's diary—the man was mad! But the ending defies all logical explanation, and fantasy reigns triumphant. The narrator returns Filiberto's body to his home, perplexed by what he has read in his friend's diary.

> Antes de que pudiera introducir la llave en la cerradura, la puerta se abrió. Apareció un indio amarillo, en bata de casa, con bufanda. Su aspecto no podía ser más repulsivo; despedía un olor a loción barata; su cara, polveada, quería cubrir las arrugas; tenía la boca embarrada de lápiz mal aplicado, y el pelo daba la impresión de estar teñido.
> —Perdone . . . no sabía que Filiberto hubiera . . . .
> —No importa; lo sé todo. Dígale a los hombres que lleven el cadaver al sótano.   [80:67]

Chac Mool is not the fantastic hallucination of a madman, but a reality who avenges himself by taking Filiberto's life before he loses his own. Fuentes, in a brief plot summary of his story, states that Chac

Mool chased Filiberto from his home to meet his death in Acapulco and that "in the end the owner replaces the god in the flea market" [51:286].

The presence of death as a theme is obvious in "Chac Mool" from the first line to the last. Here again, as in the stories of Rosario Castellanos, we see an expression of the cult of death of pre-Conquest Mexico. Chac Mool's powers have not been diminished by modern civilization. He is still capable of commanding human sacrifice, of imposing ancient ritual upon modern civilization, and of divesting man of his free will. As Emmanuel Carballo points out, Chac Mool represents "el empuje de la sangre indígena sobre la española, el peso de lo antiguo sobre lo moderno" [81:16]. "'The past, in Mexico,' says Fuentes, 'weighs heavily, because although the Conquerors, the Spaniards, carried the day, Mexico, because of its particular political and historical makeup, has given the final victory to the conquered. . . .Here the defeated have been glorified. Why? Because Mexico is a country where only the dead are heroes. . . . Our heroes are heroes because they were sacrificed. In Mexico the only saving fate is sacrifice. . . .The nostalgia for the past in Mexico is a direct result of the original defeat' "[51: 284]. Thus, Fuentes expresses the important influence of the cult of death upon modern Mexican society.

The world presented in "Chac Mool" is a curious mixture of both pre-Hispanic and modern Mexican elements. To quote Emmanuel Carballo, "los hombres que pueblan este universo se debaten entre dos teogonías que en vez de excluirse se complementan: la azteca y la católica" [82,I:xxx]. Early in this story Fuentes observes the complementary nature of these two religions upon which modern Mexican society is based.

> . . . si no fuera mexicano, no adoraría a Cristo, y—No, mira parece evidente. Llegan los españoles y te proponen adores a Dios, muerto hecho un coágulo, con el costado herido clavado en una cruz. Sacrificado. Ofrendado. ¿Qué cosa más natural que aceptar un sentimiento tan cercano a todo tu ceremonial, a toda tu vida? . . . Figúrate, en cambio, que México hubiera sido conquistado por budistas o mahometanos. No es concebible que nuestros indios veneraran a un individuo que murió de indigestión. Pero un

Dios al que no Ie basta que se sacrifiquen por él, sino que incluso va a que Ie arranquen el corazón, ¡caramba!, jaque mate a Huitzilopochtli! El cristianismo, en su sentido cálido sangriento, de sacrificio y liturgia, se vuelve una prolongación natural y novedosa de la religión indígena. Los aspectos de caridad, amor y la otra mejilla, en cambio, son rechazados. Y todo en México es eso, hay que matar a los hombres para poder creer en ellos.   [80:58]

Here, then, we find that the cult of death is not only manifested in the characterization and action of the story, but is also examined from the sociological point of view. Fuentes stresses the all-important role of the cult of death as the common denominator between the Mexican and Spanish cultures which enabled their relatively effortless fusion and provided the basis for modern Mexican society. As Emir Rodríguez Monegal points out, "el mismo Fuentes ha subrayado su intento de explorar en ellos [the short stories of *Los dias enmascarados*] la superviviencia de viejas culturas en el mundo mexicano" [83:146]. Undoubtedly, the outstanding feature of these old cultures was the cult of death. It is therefore the survival of this phenomenon which is often reflected in Fuentes' works.

Very similar to "Chac Mool" is the fifth story of the collection, "Por boca de los dioses." Once again, a work of art gains control of the protagonist and brings about his death. Oliverio, aficionado of painting, engages in an argument with his friend don Diego over the merits of a work of modern art by Tamayo, displayed in the entrance of the Palacio de Bellas Artes. As a result of that argument, Oliverio rips the mouth from the painting and in response to old don Diego's objections, throws him from a window to be smashed on the pavement below. As he leaves the building with the stolen mouth, he sees a beggar woman who appears to be the reincarnation of the colonial painting which don Diego had preferred and admired. Eventually, the mouth superimposes itself upon Oliverio's and gains control of him, forcing him to do things that he does not want to do. It leads him to a basement where there are many Indian gods. Oliverio flees and locks himself in his room, but he is followed there by the goddess Tlazol whom he has met before in the hotel, and she kills him after biting off the Tamayo mouth which had adhered itself to his.

"Por boca de los dioses" contains a plethora of situations and events symbolic of modern Mexican society, which Fuentes often openly censures. He censures, among other things, the violent, pugnacious, and yet impotent nature of the Mexican, a nature which has previously been linked to the cult of death. He describes Mexico as an "armazón suntuoso de la carne muerta, oscura, pantanosa que va chupando palabras y quehaceres" [84:271].

Beatriz Espejo y Díaz interprets the overriding symbol of this story as being "el gran arraigo que ejercen sobre nosotros el arte y la teogonía indias" [84:272]. But the tone Fuentes imparts in this story, and to a lesser degree in "Chac Mool," indicates an air of disapproval of the cult of death, which is in contrast to the essentially objective presentation of the phenomenon in the short stories of the other authors discussed herein. Fuentes criticizes the fatalism, impotence, and meaningless violence of Mexican society. His works are a call for action as opposed to stoic resignation. Fuentes' predilection toward the theme of death attests to the degree to which the cult of death is an inherent part of his culture. But by his apparent censuring of certain elements of the phenomenon, he surpasses his contemporaries, who generally manifest the phenomenon in their literature but fail to dissect it and examine it with the critical eyes of the sociologist as does Carlos Fuentes.

The fame of two of the authors in this chapter is based exclusively upon the short story. One of these is Guadalupe Dueñas. As she states, "Publiqué en 1958 un libro de cuentos que alcanzó cierto éxito y desde entonces no he publicado para no opacar mi fama" [85:360]. The one book of short stories to which she alludes, *Tiene la noche un árbol*, won for its author Guadalajara's Premio José María Vigil for having been judged the best book of 1959. Since then, stories by Guadalupe Dueñas have been included in dozens of anthologies, and they have appeared frequently in all of the literary journals of Mexico and in the most important newspapers of the country. She served as a collaborator in the journal *Abside* and in other journals and magazines with large circulations. Her works in journals of other Latin American countries and of Spain are numerous; some of her stories have been translated for United States journals, and her stories were translated into English for publication by an important London publishing house.

Of the twenty-five short stories included in *Tiene la noche un árbol*, the one that is most often included in anthologies is "La historia de

Mariquita," one of the many stories of the collection that strongly manifest the cult of death. It is the story of Mariquita, first-born of five sisters, and her rather bizarre family with whom she lives for twenty years, encased in a chile bottle filled with a mixture of aguardiente and caustic soda; for Mariquita had died at birth. The story is narrated by the eldest of her four sisters. It relates how the girls' father installed Mariquita in her liquid environment shortly after her death, and how it was decided that her permanent abode should be in the room of her sisters, in order to avoid the questions and disapproval of visitors. As is indicated by the first two lines of the story, Mariquita's influence upon the lives of the other members of her family is immense. "Nunca supe por qué nos mudábamos de casa con tanta frecuencia," her sister tells us. "Siempre nuestra mayor preocupación era establecer a Mariquita" [86:23]. Thus we see that in Guadalupe Dueñas' world, too, the dead weigh heavily upon the living.

After the death of their parents, the girls continue to move from house to house, finally renting an old, decaying estate which they find most agreeable and to whose supernatural inhabitants they soon accustom themselves. "La casa se veía muy alegre; pero así y todo había duendes. En los excepcionales minutos de silencio ocurrían derrumbes innecesarios, sorprendentes bailoteos de candiles y paredes, o inocentes quebraderos de trastos y cristales. Las primeras veces revisábamos minuciosamente los cuartos, después nos fuimos acostumbrando, y cuando se repetían estos dislates no hacíamos caso" [86:26].

But Mariquita is a problem. On her account, her innocent sisters have become the objects of malicious gossip, and she herself is accused of haunting the neighborhood. "Las sirvientas inventaron que la culpable era la niña que escondíamos en el ropero: que en las noches su fantasma recorría el vecindario. Corrió la voz y el compromiso de las explicaciones; como todas éramos solteras con bastante buena reputación se puso el caso muy difícil. Fueron tantas las habladurias que la única decente result ser la niña del bote a la que siquiera no levantaron calumnias" [86:26-27].

Her sisters seek a solution to these problems, but in the meantime, Mariquita's upkeep is terribly neglected. "Mientras tanto la criatura, que llevaba tres años sin cambio de agua, se había sentado en el fondo del frasco definitivamente aburrida" [86:27]. So, finally, after twenty years, Mariquita is buried in the garden of the old estate. But she is not forgotten:

> Ahora hemos vuelto a mudarnos y no puedo olvidar el prado que encarcela su cuerpecito. Me preocupa saber si existe alguien que cuide el verde Limbo donde habita y si en las tardes todavía la arrullan las palomas.
>
> Cuando contemplo el entrañable estuche que la guardó viente años, se me nubla el corazón de nostalgia como el de aquellos que conservan una jaula vacia; se me agolpan las tristezas que viví frente a su sueño; reconstruyo mi soledad y descubro que esta niña ligó mi infancia a su muda compañia. [86:27]

Many of Guadalupe Dueñas' stories tell of childhood encounters with death. In addition to "La historia de Mariquita," there is, for example, the story of "El moribundo," in which the narrator recounts as her most enduring childhood memory the long suffering and death of a beloved friend who contracted tuberculosis while in prison for giving aid to the Cristeros. Upon the request of his family, long-time friends of her parents, he has come to spend his dying days in her home. The story provides not only a graphic description of the young man's slow demise, but also masterfully describes a young girl's first encounter with death.

"El sapo" and "Los piojos" are stories of the naive sadism of children as they inflict death by torture upon the creatures for which the stories are named. Two of the stories of the collection, "Tiene la noche un árbol" and "Al roce de la sombra," combine death and intrigue. In "Al roce de la sombra," for example, a young girl is murdered because she witnesses the mad pleasures of the two elderly and impoverished sisters with whom she has come to live.

"Judit" is the story of a young girl whose excessive pride causes her to devise a suicide pact with her boyfriend by which she intends to triumph over interfering townsfolk.

> ¿Por qué doblegarse? Ella no era bien de Ramiro, ni de nadie, para que la tomaran cuando les viniera en gana. ¿Qué sabían de su conveniencia? ¿Por qué Ie decían que por

su bien? Nadie hubiera dicho una palabra si se le hubiera ocurrido voluntariamente ser de Ramiro; también eso estaba en el orden de las cosas.

—Que hagan su gusto. Seré de él, pero no aquí. Moriremos los dos. ¡Nos hubieran dejado hablar! Aman su ruido, quieren decidir por nosotros, ser más que nosotros. No les importa más que el acontecimiento, que si yo cediera, igual los decepcionaría; en cambio, así les daremos la gran función. Por mucho tiempo hablarán de los dos. [86:118-19]

But, as she holds the dead Ramiro in her arms, pride and self-love provide her with the rationalization she needs to excuse herself from carrying out the pact. "Es mejor que yo viva para prolongar el dolor de tu muerte" [86:121]. "Judit," then, is essentially a story of pride; and as such, it well illustrates the point that in Mexico pride and death very often walk hand-in-hand.

Finally, in "Las ratas" and "Guía en la muerte," Guadalupe Dueñas deals with the age-old theme of mortal corruption, the fate of the body after death. In the former, an ex-caretaker in the Panteón de Dolores describes the efficiency of the rats of the pantheon as they devour, upon arrival, the dead who inhabit the place. The final paragraphs of this story present the narrator's twentieth-century statement of the death-the-leveler motif:

Doy una moneda al hombrecillo y procuro que mis dedos no toquen su mano. Lo veo alejarse. Su estatura no es mayor que cuando sentado lustraba mis zapatos, como si no tuviera muslos y las rodillas fueran pegadas a la caja del cuerpo; arrastrando los pies camina igual que un mono de cuerda.

Miro mis manos, mis manos perfumadas, la piel que cuido y que también será devorada, repartida en sus lívidas panzas manchadas de jiote; yo que me amo tanto y que evité el contacto del pobre bolero.   [86:107]

"Guía en la muerte" is not a fictional work, but rather an account of the guided tour through the catacombs of Guanajuato where thousands go every year to view the mummies.

In speaking of the short stories of Guadalupe Duenas, Emmanuel Carballo has stated that they are "más producto de la espontaneidad que de la reflexión" [82,I:xxi]. It has also been stated that "la autora decanta las circunstancias y suprime toda 'escenografía' accesoria, tratando de ofrecer al lector únicamente lo esencial" [87:132]. In nearly half of the stories of *Tiene la noche un árbol*, "lo esencial" is death. The fact that the expression of this theme is a spontaneous one on the part of the author serves as further evidence that the cult of death is still an integral part of the Mexican psyche and that, as such, it is freely manifested in Mexican literature.

Eraclio Zepeda's fame, like that of Guadalupe Dueñas, rests upon one volume of short stories, *Benzulul*, published in 1959. Like Rosario Castellanos', his stories are set in the primitive world of Chiapas, though Enrique Congrains Martin is of the opinion that Zepeda surpasses Castellanos with his "capacidad innata para captar lo que es esencialmente indígena" [87:212].

As an exponent of the Mexican cult of death, Zepeda also surpasses Castellanos. For, as we have seen, manifestations of the cult of death are evident in only selected stories of *Ciudad Real*, while death is a prominent theme in each of the eight short stories of *Benzulul*. To quote the back cover of the volume,

> *Benzulul* encierra una variada colección de psicologías primitivas, y no es casual que la muerte sea el común denominador de los ocho cuentos: el autor ha escogido esa luz funebre por creer que con ella destacaran mejor los rasgos esenciales de nuestro rostro más antiguo.
>
> Ya que para el lector son evidentes, sobre todo, los valores humanos y literarios del volumen, tal vez no será inútil señalar que también tiene interés antropológico esta sentida investigación del alma indígena.   [88]

The eight stories in this collection may be divided into three categories. The first of these contains four stories, "Benzulul," "Vientooo," "Quien dice verdad," and "Patrocinio Tipá," in which Zepeda describes the feelings and attitudes of the indigenous population of southern Mexico. The next category deals with characters and life styles that are typically mestizo. Into this category fall "El Caguamo," "El Mudo," and "La Cañada del Principio." The last story of the collection, "No se asombre, sargento," in a category of its own, participates in both realities described in the other seven stories of the collection.

The first story of the collection, and the one from which the collection takes its name, is "Benzulul." It is the story of Juan Rodríguez Benzulul, an Indian who feels himself defeated and condemned to wander the roads of Tenejapa after death because of his Indian name. He longs to possess the name of Encarnación Salvatierra, because he knows that then he could be like Encarnación, free in life to act and in death to rest, for an Indian name implies impotence and eternal unrest, while a Spanish name signifies power and eternal peace. "Los muertos sin nombre ya no guardan la semilla, dice la nana Porfiria, pero tienen que llevar hojas pa envolverla. Se les cae la semilla cuando mueren, pero tienen la obligacion de buscarla. En la noche con luna es cuando buscan las hojas. . . .Los que tienen nombre se quedan con la semilla en su lugar. Cuando yo muera voy a seguir caminando este camino: Juan Rodríguez Benzulul no dejará el camino. ¡Si consigo un nombre todo cambia! Encarnación Salvatierra va a morir sabroso. No va a aparecer en la noche. No va a espantar. No va a llorar. Tiene nombre" [88:21].

Therefore, when "la nana Porfiria" gives him Encarnación's name, Benzulul goes through the town a changed man, and he acquires a strength previously unknown to him. But Encarnación Salvatierra soon tires of Benzulul's attempt to take his name, and to prevent him from continuing in his attempt, he hangs him from a tree and cuts out his tongue.

There are many aspects to this story pertinent to our discussion of the cult of death. The first sentence of "Benzulul" establishes a relationship between man and nature that is evident throughout the entire collection. "Mientras avazanba por la vereda, una parte de su cuerpo se iba quedando en las marcas de sus huellas" [88:13]. The distinction between man and nature is blurred; the two mutually influence each other and are complementary parts of a greater whole, a cosmic process in which nothing is ever lost, but merely changed in form. Benzulul expresses this idea by means of the following metaphor: "Cuando hay un ocurrido, [el rio] lo convierte en piedrita redonda y se lo guarda en el fondo. . . . Las piedritas tán siempre guardadas y allí van creciendo. Son huevos de montaña. Cuando es el tiempo acabalado, se hacen piedrotas pa lavar ropa o pa jimbarse de cabeza al río. Después crecen más y se van a donde falte un cerro" [88:15].

The distinction between life and death is also blurred. They, too, mutually influence one another and are seen as complementary parts of a cosmic process. Benzulul's world is peopled with both the living and the dead. The nameless dead wander the roads in search of "hojas para envolver la semilla" and are especially visible by moonlight or to dogs.

> Cuando hay luna las cosas cambian. . . .Asoman cosas del fondo de los ríos. También asoman muertos. Muertos que, como el Martín, como mi tata y mi nana, que, como yo, no tuvieron nombre. Lo andan buscando pa cubrir la semilla. A mí no me gusta encontrar espantos. Pero la luna los trae al camino y el camino es de todos.
> . . .Los perros miran a los muertos.   [88:18]

The constant repetition of words or sentences that serve as a kind of *estribillo* in "Benzulul," and throughout the collection, gives to these stories and to the lives described therein a circular quality. Man, nature, life, and death are presented as complementary parts of a vast life cycle in which negative and positive labels are out of place. It is the cult of death of pre-Conquest Mexico that we see in these stories, uncontaminated by the centuries.

The intimate relationship between man and nature is a concept emphasized in each of the four stories dealing with the indigenous population of Chiapas. In each of these, and especially in "Vientooo" and "Patrocinio Tipá," it is this concept which determines the protagonist's attitude toward life and death. In "Vientooo," for example, Matías allows a snake to bite him, because there is no moon and he has been destined from birth to die by snake bite during a full moon. "Yo, mirálo, solo lo voy a morir cuando lo busque la culebra que lo mamó las chichis de mi nana cuando nací. Noche de luna es que tiene que ser, pa que me haga su efecto; pa que me haga enjundia. ¡De otro modo dónde vas a creer que yo me muera!" [88:65]

Therefore, he speaks to the snake and reaches out to stroke her, saying, "— Ya viniste, hermanita. ¿Por qué me querés llevar? Ahora que no hay luna. Sólo con luna es que me podés llevar. Que me puedo morir. ¿A quí vinistes, hermanita?" [88:77]

Even after the first bite, his faith in his destiny is unaltered.

> −¿Por qué me mordiste, hermanita? Yo te iba a acariciar.
> ¿Pero acaso te olvidaste que a mí no me podís matar? Sólo que
> fuera noche de luna podés fregarme. Y eso, yo queriendo.
>
> La nauyaca volvió a enroscarse y preparó el cuello
> nuevamente. Los ojos, pequeños dardos, y la lengua con
> movimientos lentos, primero, y muy rápidos después.
>
> −Mordéme otra . . .pa que veás. Pa que te des cuenta
> que al Matías no lo podes fregar. . . .
>
> Y acercó la mano, hasta casi rozar la cabeza triangular.
>
> Uno, dos, tres, mordidas rápidas.   [88:78]

And still, when the pain becomes severe, he refuses to take the antidote. "¿Pa qué? Si yo no puedo morir en noche oscura" [88:79]. In his agony, he notices that the south wind for which he has prayed for days comes to sweep away the rain and clouds and to reveal behind the clouds the full moon that brings with it his death.

"El Caguamo" pertains to the second category of stories in *Benzulul*. It is the story of a chain of death passed on from father to son and strengthened by a town, a people, and a way of life dedicated to the cult of violence, a product of the cult of death. Primitivo Barragán, El Caguamo, was a good man, respected, and a hard worker. And yet his father, though not a bad man, had died by the gun, and his last act had been to blow open the head of his assassin with the gun which later passed as an inheritance to his son.

Primitivo has no desire to live by violence. He merely wants to make a secure, peaceful life with his woman, Eugenia. But the town makes that impossible. They begin vicious gossip which forces Eugenia's father to seek to avenge his soiled honor. But his attempt to ambush and kill Primitivo fails, and instead Primitivo is forced, in self-defense, to kill his father-in-law with the gun he has inherited from his father. More killings follow, all unnecessary and unwanted by Primitivo. His wife can no longer bear his presence. His only hope lies in his unborn son. But Eugenia, to avenge her father, aborts herself, and Primitivo, in an act of grief-produced madness, tears open her stomach, burns his house, kills his animals, and flees. But he flees not so much to free himself from reprisals as he does to free himself from the necessity of continuing to kill. He is afraid that he will not be able to break the chain of death of which he is a link, that "they" will not allow it. "'No quero volver a hacerlo. Ese sudor pegajoso y la sangre rebotando como piedras; ese susto que da el andar matando no quero volverlo a sentir. Que me dejen quieto. Que me dejen solo y seguiré siendo hombre bueno. Ellos me hicieron creminar y pueden volver a hacerlo,' pensaba el Caguamo viendo hacia Jitotol" [88:55]. And yet, one wonders if among a people so dedicated to the cult of violence and the cult of death a man like El Caguamo can ever really escape.

El Vaquerizo, protagonist of "El Mudo," was also a man of peace. He had avoided any involvement in the Revolution that raged around him, and yet he was now facing a firing squad, because, struck mute by a fall from his horse, he could not tell the revolutionary forces the location of the guns of the Municipal Council. He did not know their location, but he was unable even to tell them that. And no one believed that he was truly unable to speak. So he died before the firing squad, and they said of him, "Se murió en su línea; en su mero relajo; era macho el Vaquerizo" [88:101].

Reality in this story assumes a nightmarish form. Life and death seem to float in a senseless vacuum. El Vaquerizo notes precisely this situation in the first pages of the story. "Vaquerizo no movió la vista de la puerta. Le parecía que toda esta situación era de a mentiras, de puro vacilón. Eso de que le digan a uno que ya mañana no va a hacer nada más que ir a poner el pecho para que lo venadeen sin oportunidad de que se defiende, como si fuera un coyote matrero, era a lo que no podía acostumbrarse el Vaquerizo" [88:86-87].

This same nightmarish quality is evident in "La Cañada del Principio," but at least in that story there is a logical motive for Neófito's presence in the senseless war arena. He is there to avenge his father's death at the hands of the federales. But that is not so with El Vaquerizo.

And yet, faced with death, no matter how absurd, and despite his previous fears and efforts to escape her, El Vaquerizo faces his destiny without fear and without any thought of escape. As Zepeda explains it, "No tenía ya esperanzas; tampoco temor; no le temblaron las piernas como dicen que les pasa a los fusilados, ni le dieron ganas de llorar. No era por valentía. Nunca tuvo fama de eso; era por otra cosa. La muerte estaba allí, de cuerpo entero y para que le daba más vueltas. El llano se abría enfrente de la barda que le servía de paredón; se iba hasta más allá de los sembrados de caña y en el camino había matorrales y piedras donde esconderse. Pero el Vaquerizo no pensó en salir corriendo; en escaparse" [88:96].

A similar situation prevails in the last story and, in my opinion, the best story of the collection, "No se asombre, sargento." The protagonist of this story was afraid when his father died, and yet, because he remembers the words passed on to him as an inheritance by his dying father, the end products of a lifetime of accumulated wisdom, he loses that fear completely at the hour of his own death. "La muerte no mata," his father had told him, "lo que mata es la suerte" [88:161]. "Lo bueno aquí en el campo es saber cuando se va uno a morir; que en el campo la muerte no es más que un sucedido que a juerzas tiene que llegar y casi siempre es hasta una salida pa los problemas" [88:158]. "Acordáte siempre, nunca debes de sentirte solo; onde quiera que estes yo voy a andar contigo" [88:161].

Fathers are instruments of continuity for their sons in Zepeda's stories. From his father, Primitivo Barragán had inherited his ability as a marksman and his fate as a killer. The protagonist of "No se asombre, sargento," from his father, has learned to die.

> Ansina jué como se murió mi tata. Ansina me enseñó a morir. Ansina jué que me dijo lo que se debe hacer. . . .sé que el tata tenía razón cuando me dijo que la muerte no viene a ser más que un caballo matrero al que algún día tenemos que montar. Por eso es que estoy tranquilo señor. Y usté, sargento, también debe de estar igual. Hoy le toca tirar a usté, mañana le tocará recibir.
>
> ¡Bueno! yo ya acabé de hacer la tumba. No más le recomiendo que me entierren hasta el fondo. Usté dice, sargento, en dónde me pongo pa que me fusile. [88:163-4]

Confronted by imminent death, the protagonist of "No se asombre, sargento" discusses with spontaneous familiarity the phenomenon and the counsel given him by his dying father. As Enrique Congrains Martin points out, "La muerte como una experiencia natural, normal, 'como un sucedido que a juerzas tiene que llegar,' es la idea que sostiene el protagonista, encarnando una actitud vital muy arraigada en el campesinado mexicano" [87:212].

Man faced with death is a theme that appears in all of the stories of *Benzulul*. It is the last story of the collection, though, that best expresses the attitude toward death that prevails throughout the work.

There is no question that the bases of the Mexican cult of death lie in both indigenous Mexican and pre-Conquest Spanish culture and that the fusion of these two cultures created the somewhat extreme social phenomenon that is very much alive and evident in Mexico today. With regard to the fusion of cultures, though, there is one significant feature we must point out. Clara Passafari de Gutierrez, in discussing the works of Juan Rulfo, has stated that "Rulfo no presenta la vida de Mexico sino el alma mexicana en lo más hondo de su atavismo" [70:75]. The cult of death is an outstanding element of that soul, and in almost all of the stories discussed herein, we find that it appears to be a phenomenon that reverts not to an earlier Catholic prototype, but to early indigenous culture. Thus, R. A. M. VanZantwijk tells us that "the introduction of Christianity into Mexico was the logical consequence of the Aztec view of life. Christianity is thus, as far as confessed by Indians, taken in the Aztec religious sense and as such has never been, and never will be, able to free itself from their beliefs" [7:114]. The Aztec attitude toward death, then, was refined and augmented by the Christian counterpart; but the phenomenon that one sees reflected in most of the stories in this volume, though it owes its survival and development to the fusion of Christian and indigenous attitudes, in reality exhibits a far closer kinship to the latter.

Nevertheless, we've seen that the phenomenon was an outstanding element not only of ancient, indigenous Mexican literature, but of pre-Conquest Spanish literature, and of the Mexican short story of the period 1947-60. The six authors discussed in this chapter represent the major regions of Mexico and thereby illustrate, in addition, that the cult of death is by no means a purely regional phenomenon, but is one that manifests itself in the work of writers from all regions of the country.

The study of manifestations of the cult of death in the short stories of each of the six authors discussed in this chapter supports the hypothesis that the cult of death is a significant, perhaps the most significant, element of the modern Mexican psyche and that, as such, it logically manifests itself in all genres of 20th century Mexican literature. That this volume focuses on only one literary genre by no means implies that the findings herein are not equally applicable to the novel, to poetry, and to other genres.

I leave it to younger scholars to evaluate in detail the degree to which manifestations of the cult of death have been a significant feature of the Mexican short story since 1960. Certainly, there was a tendency among younger, post-sixties writers to move away from a conscientious attempt to express "the Mexican" toward an expression of more universal themes. Cosmopolitan settings and mentalities were explored where, during the fifties, the concern was more for the rural. It was as if earlier writers had discovered and revealed the nature and source of the Mexican character, and younger writers were turning to more universal themes in an attempt to extend themselves beyond the limits of their nationality. For example, young writers like Gustavo Sáinz and José Agustín attempted, for the first time in Mexico, to reveal in literature the world of the adolescent. And the human problems dealt with in post-sixties short stories were of a more complex nature than those basic problems of survival, life, and death dealt with in earlier works. Social problems were also of a more complex nature than those formerly dealt with, which tended to be rural problems, like the Indian and agrarian reform.

The post-sixties writers were a more self-searching group. They were concerned less with revealing their nature as Mexicans than with revealing their nature as individuals in the more universal sense, and in their writing they appear to have been conscientiously seeking a *sui generis* form. There is an evident bitter humor and cynicism in many of their works and, especially significant, a snobbism which was completely lacking in the literature of most of the writers of the fifties whose works are discussed in this chapter.

It is worth noting that Carlos Fuentes also followed in this direction. As noted earlier, the tone Fuentes imparts in many of his works indicates an air of disapproval of the cult of death, which is in contrast to the essentially objective presentation of the phenomenon in the short stories of Rulfo and others. Fuentes' predilection toward the theme of death attests to the degree to which the cult of death is an inherent part of his culture, but his apparent censuring of certain elements of the phenomenon leads him in a direction more consistent with the post-sixties generation

However, even when Fuentes appears to embrace European over Mexican themes, as when, in 1962, he penned perhaps the most Gothic of Mexican novellas, *Aura*, he cannot escape incorporating elements of the Mexican cult of death in his writing. The setting of this work is a dark and mysterious mansion, paneled in dark wood, carved in Gothic style, in the old center of Mexico City, to which a young, impoverished historian has gone in answer to an ad for employment. His job seems straight forward: to write the memoirs of the deceased husband of the decrepit owner. But nothing about the situation the narrator finds himself in is straight forward. The labyrinthine mansion exudes an atmosphere of mystery and suspense; the narrator's senses are bombarded by hallucinatory scenes like the wailing of cats, whose existence his employer denies, though he later sees them writhing in flames outside his window in a garden the existence of which is also denied by the old crone. And then there is Aura, the old woman's companion, whose mysterious existence creates the emotional framework within which the narrator moves from passion to anger to terror and, finally, to total abandonment . . . high, overwrought emotions typical of the Gothic novel. The novella concludes with the engendering of doubles—the old crone and Aura are one and the same; the narrator and the old woman's deceased husband are one—death and mortality are defied, at least for a while longer.

There appears to be little of the Mexican cult of death in this novella and much of the classical Gothic. There is no reflection of the deterministic and fatalistic acceptance of death that so typifies the Mexican cult of death; however, there is also no return to the logical and rational here, nor any hint of damnation, which lends this work, despite its cosmopolitan trappings, a Mexican rather than European air.

Generally speaking, then, one might say that, due to the more subjective and universal nature of the post-sixties Mexican short story, manifestations of the cult of death became a less prominent element of the genre than they were previously, or at least they were present in a far more subtle form.

This is not to say that there did not exist young writers who followed in the tradition of established artists like Juan Rulfo, José Revueltas, or Rosario Castellanos, for there were many. An outstanding example among these is Tomás Mojarro, who was called an "heredero directo" of Rulfo, Yañez, and Revueltas [70:214]. Nevertheless, one must take into account the ascendency of a new group of writers whose concerns were more cosmopolitan, more universal, and in whose writings manifestations of the cult of death were less prevalent.

That said, we must not forget that as a social phenomenon the cult of death is still of supreme significance in Mexico. It seems certain that as new scholars examine post-sixties short story production in Mexico, they will find that, despite new tendencies, manifestations of the cult of death abound.

I realized what had happened. In death, I had become a Mexican.

Carlos Fuentes, *The Orange Tree*

5

From Sacrificial Fire to Fire in the Mind: The Mexican Cult of Death in Contemporary Literature and Politics

We have clearly established that death and violence—often revolutionary violence—are dominant leitmotifs in modern Mexican literature. And we have established that both themes can be linked to a cult of death, the roots of which are buried deep in the ancient past and serve as a vital key to understanding the Mexican worldview, then and now.

For post-revolutionary thinkers like Octavio Paz and his contemporaries, the cult of death was a uniquely Mexican phenomenon, one that constituted their greatest expression of cultural nationalism and, perhaps, their surest path to a resurrection of power. The search for the essence of national identity that dominated Mexican arts and letters during much of the 20th century focused on incorporating the indigenous heritage into mainstream systems and worldview, a process that is still ongoing.

The Mexican cult of death lies at the heart of the earliest processes of civilisation building in Meso-America. Ancient Mexicans believed that the gods had created a succession of worlds before this world came into being and that, one by one, they had destroyed each. This world was to meet the same fate as its predecessors. Creation was steeped in death.

In Aztec mythology, the world was created through the blood and sacrifice of the gods, whose immolation by fire and air brought light and movement to the void. In this myth of creation through sacrifice lay the latent seed from which would spring, years later, a bloody religious ritual based on the rationalisation that "if only the death of the gods could make possible the movement and life of the Sun, then only the sacrifice of men, who play the role of gods on earth, can maintain its life and motion" [4:31] Only through self-sacrifice could humanity postpone the cataclysms that were destined to put an end to the Sun and preserve it from the same destiny of its predecessors.

In Maya mythology, global destruction was linked with an obsession with time, to which the Maya assigned a supernatural or magical content. Though distinct in some ways, the Maya cult of death reflects the same deterministic and fatalistic world view possessed by other Meso-Americans.

As a dominant theme in Ancient Mexican literature, the cult of death finds its clearest expression in the lyric poetry of the philosopher-kings. Here we find the most personal expression of the existence of the phenomenon in the indigenous Mexican psyche.

As Garibay tells us, we see the enigma of death, inevitable and unique, cast its shadow over every song of Anahuac. As if the obsession with death, elevated by myth to the quality of a sacrificial act, was that which most overwhelmed those consciousnesses [10:I, 195]. The cult of death reflected in contemporary Mexican literature is, without a doubt, the child of that ancient, indigenous obsession.

By the last decade of the twentieth century, the Mexican cult of death had reestablished itself as a dominant literary, artistic and social theme. Much as it had during the half century following the Mexican Revolution, the phenomenon became associated with efforts to build a new political consciousness, confront the continued alienation of vast segments of the Mexican population from the mainstream, and assert national identity by returning to the roots of the Mexican psyche.

In 1994, Carlos Fuentes published *The Orange Tree*, a collection of five novellas in which he returned to themes reminiscent of those he had incorporated into his first work, *Los días enmascarados*, themes that clearly reflect key aspects of the Mexican cult of death: belief in the unity of cosmic and terrestrial forces, circular and static time, the

Mexican preoccupation with the idea of duality (life-death, past-present, spiritual-sensual, and so on).

> Then, from the bottom of the lagoon, unexpectedly, there surges up a chorus of voices, which at first we two brothers can't manage to understand . . . One sings in Nahuatl, another in Castilian, but they end up blending together; one sings the unfolding of the flower-like Quetzal mantles, another the swaying of the Sevillian poplars in the breeze; one begs that the flowers not die, that they last in someone's hands; another, that the wounded, love-struck crane not die . . . The voices fuse to sing together in the fleeting passage of life; they wonder if they've come in vain, we pass through the earth: we touch the flowers, we touch the fruit, but a loud, disconsolate scream remembers, adding another voice to the group: Within the garden I shall die, within the rose garden shall I be slain, words that fuse with the responsory of the Indian land, No one, no one, no one, in truth, lives in the land: we've only come to a dream, and the words flow far from the valley, into a distant sea where the silent rivers of life come to a halt; We, says the Nahuatl voice, shall have to go to the place of mystery . . . And then, as if borne along by a wind that scatters the pestilential smoke and puts out the cruel lights and silences the strident noises, the singing ends without ending:
>
> My flowers will never end,
> My songs will never end.
> I raise them up,
> I am only a singer . . .   [90:80-81]

The image of the sacrificial hero god is a dominant one in the works of other contemporary Mexican writers as well.

Nationalist renderings of the martyred hero, and of the theme of death in general, while attempting to inspire a new political consciousness, also reinforce a cult of death born of the ancient world view.

This blending of a new political consciousness with ancient myth and lore is found thoughout 20th century Mexican literature. Man faced with death is a theme that appears in all of the stories discussed in the previous chapter, and the attitude toward death that prevails throughout those works is one that clearly harks back to ancient indigenous roots.

Over centuries, though, the cult of death as a purely indigenous phenomenon has been altered, first by the imposition of foreign religious beliefs, then by adaptation to modern political tenets. The fusion of indigenous and invading cultures served to intensify a social phenomenon that was at the heart of the ancient world view, leaving us today with socio-political phenomena like the cult of Santa Muerte, the skeletal saint, who has become the protector and symbol of power for the barrio gang members and felons of Mexico City and has become somewhat of a mascot for the revolutionary PRD political party. The cult of Santa Muerte has seen a revival in the past decades, which Mexican writer and poet Homero Aridjis attributes to disillusionment with "the system." "There is a complete disappointment with the government," he states, "people can't expect anything from the politicans, the parties or the established Church" [91].

In Mexico, the imposition of Spanish Catholicism reinforced and, to some extent, redirected expressions of the indigenous cult of death. In recent revolutionary writings, we clearly see expression of the cult of death of ancient origin blended with a new political consciousness.

A brief analysis of *Shadows of Tender Fury*, a compilation of letters and communiques of Subcomandante Marcos and the Zapatista Army for National Liberation, reveals a newly emerging, Mexican (indeed, American) world-view into which reflections of the Mexican cult of death are fully incorporated.

Marcos best reveals that process of incorporation in a piece of writing he completed in 1992 "to waken the conscience of some compañeros who were then thinking of joining our struggle" [92:31]. The piece, entitled "Chiapas: The Southeast in Two Winds, A Storm, and A Prophesy," tells how the voices of the past are repeated today, and how "the Indians will begin to walk again, together with other dispossessed marchers, but this time with surer steps, in order to take what belongs to them. And how death's music, which now plays only for those who have nothing, will play for others too" [92:47].

It is the Ancient Mexican past to which Marcos here refers, a past that reveals the formation of a collective memory into which is incorporated the Mexican cult of death and the unique world-view from which it derives.

In the chapter entitled "Already Talking About Memories," Marcos reveals themes that may well have come directly from ancient lyric poetry, as he, too, celebrates "death in battle or on the sacrificial stone" and the memory of those who nurture life and a new world with their blood:

> A lot of us burned our ships in the early dawn of the 1st of January and started down this hard road, ski-masks covering our faces. We took a one-way path that permits no return, knowing that at the end, death and not triumph probably awaits us. And what would triumph be? Seizing power? No, something even harder to win: a new world. [. . .] But, . . .we decided a long time ago, and not without pain, that we had to make ourselves strong in the face of the death of those at our side who were falling, dying with honour to be sure, but dying nonetheless. [. . .] And we understand . . . that in the middle of the blood [. . .], there is a simple truth: we are invincible, we cannot lose [. . .] we do not deserve to lose. But as we say here, our job is this: to fight and to die so that others may live, so that they may live better lives, much better lives, than the ones we now leave behind.
> [92:109-110]

Though Marcos's words may reveal little of the fatalism that characterised Ancient Mexican thought, they clearly reveal the dualism that constitutes the very basis of the Mexican cult of death.

That dualism is reflected as well in a 1994 communique from the EZLN to the indigenous peoples cast out of their lands and their history. It demands "the unconditional return of all displaced peoples to their legitimate lands and the punishment of those who oppress their own race and bleed their own brothers," and states that "this demand has an important place on the path to a world of justice and truth that will have to be born out of our death" [92:146-147].

With Marcos's poetry we come full circle in our analysis of manifestations of the Mexican cult of death in myth and literature. In a poem entitled "PROBLEMS", he writes:

> beneath this land there is country too
> and no one hears us,
> and we open our hearts
> (because one always opens one's heart
> when no one is listening)
> and we tell
> (our country)
> the small hard story
> of those who went on dying
> to love her,
> and who are no longer here to agree with me,
> but they agree even without being here,
> those who taught us
> that one loves one's country,
> for example,
> amidst gunfire
> and smiling.   [92:172-173]

For modem Mexicans, as for their predecessors, creation, the creation of a new world, is steeped in death. But, though the new world may be born of death, it may no longer be doomed to catastrophe. Fatalism, as an aspect of the Mexican cult of death, was a necessary tool of the ancient priest-politicians, one that was clearly reflected in lyric poetry and other literary forms. Hope may become the dominant theme of twenty-first century Mexican letters, as indigenous Mexican cultures and world-view are, for the fIrst time since the Conquest, fully integrated into the mainstream. Yet, as a general cultural context the Mexican cult of death will survive. Manifestations of the cult of death are evident in the earliest indigenous myth and literature, and they will continue to be reflected in literature of every genre as long as the indigenous soul remains alive in Mexico.

I hope the leaving is joyful; and I hope never to return.

Frida Kahlo

6

The Mexican Cult of Death in the Life and Art of Frida Kahlo: Exposing the Mexican Psyche to the World

Frida Kahlo discovered—probably inadvertently—a unique yet replicable means of utilizing art as a means of insinuating key aspects of indigenous culture and world view into the collective psyche of modern mainstream society. Her work was neither folk art nor the totally subjective expression of personal suffering and angst to which many of her critics allude. It was, instead, a means by which she softened her personal suffering by subsuming it within a pre-modern world view, born of ancient Mexican cultures and preserved in traditional Mexican cultures today. A byproduct of her personal quest was that her art insinuated the essence of the traditional Mexican world view into the minds and hearts of all who viewed it, leading them into a deeper, if subliminal, understanding of the culture from which it derived. Her art stands as an interesting alternative to traditional folk art, which tends to represent to its viewers something that is decidedly "foreign," if pleasant to the eye.

Rarely, if ever, were key aspects of indigenous cultures integrated into mainstream colonial institutions. Native peoples were alienated and isolated from the mainstream, foreign culture and, often, from their own culture and worldview. The psychological and systemic effects of this cultural partition were grave for all concerned. They have served as the single greatest impediment to achieving nationhood.

The 20th century brought about an era of cultural nationalism that called for an end to the cultural partition of the past and the integration of indigenous cultures into the mainstream as a means of creating, at last, a true national identity.

Frida Kahlo serves as example par excellence of the power of one artist's inner vision to introduce key aspects of indigenous culture and world view into the collective psyche of a nation divided against itself. As such, she may serve as a valuable study for aboriginal artists everywhere.

In Frida's art, visions of key elements of the indigenous world view are so tactfully and ingeniously insinuated into imagery from the mainstream culture that even the best known of her critics have been unable to discern it, though they, along with all who view her art, incorporate those symbols into their own slowly evolving world view and national identity.

Manifestations of the Mexican cult of death are an aspect of Frida Kahlo's art that has been overlooked by her biographers; one that I think provides an important alternative perspective on her life and work, and one that, through her international exhibits, allowed Frida to expose to the world a key aspect of the Mexican psyche.

In the many biographies of Frida, preeminent among which is that of Hayden Herrera, whose work provided the basis for the screenplay of the movie *Frida*, none has alluded directly to a dominant theme in her life and works, the Mexican Cult of Death. All have alluded to and attempted to explain the profusion of death-related scenes and symbols in her works, but none has seen them as symbols of truth and power for Frida as a Mexican artist and activist, and for Mexicans as a people.

Frida Kahlo spent most of her adult life reinventing herself in her art. "I never painted dreams," she wrote. "I painted my own reality" [94:ix]. The reality she painted, and created, reflects her personal search for identity and immortality. As importantly, it reflects the efforts of a people, the Mexican people, to create a collective identity, a national psyche, by which they, too, after a half millennium, might rediscover the path to immortality.

As an individual, Frida Kahlo had little to which she could say she truly belonged. She was neither culturally nor physically whole. Though half Mexican (Spanish/Indian) on her mother's side, her photographer father, from whom she inherited her talent as an artist, was an epileptic German Jew. Through a series of unfortunate diseases and accidents, Frida herself became isolated in a world of pain and physical deterioration that was destined to end her life tragically and prematurely. Those same physical limitations prevented her from immortalizing herself through motherhood. Even her marriage to Diego Rivera in 1929 cast her into a relationship in which she often assumed the role of outsider, neither capable of deflecting her husband's legendary absorption in himself and his work nor of keeping him faithful.

To survive, and thrive, in the face of both physical and psychological adversity, Frida chose to mythify herself; first, in her life and, later, in her art. As a teenager she chose to fully identify herself with the most significant historical movement in modern Mexican history, the Mexican Revolution. To this end, she changed her year of birth from 1907 to 1910, so that out of the labor pains from which modern Mexico was born, a new Frida was born as well. Mexico's struggle to identify the cultural and psychological forces that would define *mexicanidad* for the future became Frida's struggle to rise above her own solitude and mortality by becoming a Mexican archetype.

The search for the essence of *mexicanidad* dominated Mexican arts and letters throughout the first half of the twentieth century. Historian E. Bradford Burns associates that search with "a wave of cultural nationalism" that swept the hemisphere. "The intellectuals, long slavish imitators of European styles, turned their backs on their former mentors to seek the indigenous roots of national culture," he explains. "They probed national psychology, questioned national motives, and reexamined the past . . . . A Latin American renaissance in art, literature, music, and dance resulted from these proddings. It originated in Mexico" [93:201].

During that time, men of letters like Octavio Paz strove to identify those forces in the Mexican psyche behind which Mexicans shielded themselves from the pain of defeat and solitude, but through which they would some day emerge once again whole. The great muralists Rivera, Siqueiros and Orozco, reintroduced the glories and tragedies of indigenous culture to a Mexico that for centuries chose to shun its indigenous heritage in favor of imported systems and worldviews. All turned to indigenous culture as the prime symbol of America and American-ness.

In this respect Frida's search for her own and Mexico's collective identity in indigenous myths and archetypes is consistent with the artistic and intellectual movement of which she was part. However, Frida clearly chose those myths and archetypes that best reflected her own needs and suffering. Biographer Hayden Herrera suggests that, for Frida, painting was a form of psychological surgery. Her husband, Diego Rivera, described her art as "individual-collective" and monumentally realistic to the point whereby it allowed her to paint "at the same time the exterior and interior of herself and the world" [95: 260]. From that art, replete with severed hearts, flowing blood, skeletons and skulls, it is apparent that that aspect of the Mexican psyche with which Frida most identified and in which she perhaps found greatest solace was the Mexican cult of death.

El culto a la muerte, the Mexican cult of death, is a term that readily calls to the mind of anyone familiar with Mexico and her culture the unusually constant place of death in the minds and lives of the Mexican people. Death is, so to speak, a constant companion of the Mexican in his or her journey through life. Octavio Paz described the phenomenon well when he observed that "the word death is not pronounced in New York, in Paris, in London, because it burns the lips. The Mexican, in contrast, is familiar with death, jokes about it, caresses it, sleeps with it, celebrates it; it is one of his favorite toys and his most steadfast love" [97:57].

The roots of the Mexican cult of death are buried deep in the soil formed by the union of two distinct cultures, one indigenous American and the other European, each of which possessed a perceptible cult of death and each of which imparted certain aspects of that cult to the culture of which it was co-creator. Frida Kahlo's *mexicanidad,* which she expressed both in her outward appearance and in her highly personal art, was further enhanced by her having been, herself, the product of a Mexican-European union. The cult of death, then, was not only a salient theme in her art; it was a means by which she could better come to grips with her own cultural duality.

Frida identified passionately with her Mexican roots. Fused with the highly personal and psychological elements in her art are strong elements of Mexican tradition, both Catholic and pre-Columbian. Frida never wrote about her use of pre-Columbian iconography, but she incorporated dominant symbols, many of them associated with the cult of death, into her rendering of her personal experiences. According to Herrera, Frida Kahlo's peculiar passion for indigenous Mexican culture comes from the way it is linked with the exigencies and intensities of her life. Clearly, the Mexican cult of death was one Mexican tradition with which Frida could easily identify.

For ancient Mexicans, death lacked the fearful finality that it has in Western cultures; from their earliest myths of creation, Mexicans saw death as indivisibly linked to life. Together, these two states of being created the whole of the natural order of things.

As an awareness of death permeated every aspect of the life of the ancient Mexicans, it is understandable that it provided the motive for some their finest art. Since life came out of death as the young plant comes from the moldering seed of the earth, death was quite logically a major preoccupation of the great ancient Mexican artists.

An awareness of death permeated every aspect of Frida Kahlo's life as well. By embracing the Mexican cult of death, and the world view from which it derived, it is probable that she was able to free herself from the Western concept of death as opposed to life and come to see her own tragic circumstances in a more positive light. Herrera suggests that Frida's "preoccupation with her roots in Mexico's past . . . may have been heightened by the renewed realization that she would leave no progeny to link her with future generations" [95:219]. During those years when she painted such works as *My Nurse and I* and *Four Inhabitants of Mexico,* "the ethic of *Mexicanidad* pervaded Frida's existence on many levels: it was a style, a political stance, and a psychological support. It expressed itself in her behavior and her appearance, in the decoration of her home, and in her art" [95:219].

I suggest that it also inspired her to see that through her death and art she could nourish life and achieve the immortality that comes not from pitting the personal ego against the world but from seeing the real self as inseparable from the primordial reality and origin of all things. The frequent juxtaposition of death and fertility symbols in her work suggest her striving to understand and cope not just with her own painful existence but with the failure of the Western intellectual tradition to provide an adequate base on which human beings can meaningfully live. The theme of alienation from nature, society and one's self, which characterizes Western reality, is often presented in stark contrast with Ancient American themes, like the cult of death, that emphasize instead the unity of the one and the all.

One of Frida's earlier works, *LUTHER BURBANK* (1931), though a somewhat amateurish blending of modern Western portraiture and Ancient American themes, is perhaps the first clear revelation of Frida's strivings to incorporate into her life and work the salient Ancient American theme of death nurturing life, much as the young plant emerges from the moldering seed.

MY NURSE AND I (1937) clearly depicts the nurturing quality of Mexico's indigenous heritage. A double self-portrait is suggested, in which Frida's Indian aspect nurtures the other and provides a life-sustaining force with strong reflections of the Mexican cult of death. Herrera suggests that the nurse's Teotihuacan funerary mask "threatens Frida's life" [95:220]. I suggest that the opposite is true; that, as a "sacrificial victim," Frida saw herself as able to transcend ordinary reality and, through her death and suffering, become part of an eternal cosmic whole.

FOUR INHABITANTS OF MEXICO (1938) combines Frida's and Mexico's preoccupation with death, again, within the context of the Mexican cult of death, which is represented as one of the basic components of the Mexican psyche.

The clay skeleton, symbolic of Day of the Dead festivities, emerges as the dominant figure in this work. It looms white and bright in the foreground, overshadowing the Diego-inspired Judas figure to its right and dwarfing the straw man and burro that symbolize daily Mexican existence.

Herrera tells us that Frida referred to the skeleton as "very gay." Yet, she describes the painting as "a somewhat ambivalent celebration of [Frida's] Mexican roots," and tells us that the artist, "rather than ignoring the sorrows of her native land, identifies them with her own" [96:24].

It might be, instead, that the "gay" skeleton affirms Frida's strivings to adopt the Eastern-based indigenous worldview from which the Mexican cult of death derives as a means of better coping with anxiety and isolation born of her own unique circumstances and a collective Western consciousness.

The Diego-Judas, wired to entertain as it is destroyed; the broken fertility idol, symbolic of Frida's *in*fertility; and the straw man, who represents the fragile, transitory nature of all life become insignificant as symbols of individual or collective angst when juxtaposed with the bright gay symbol of death that signifies the existence of an all-encompassing, nurturing whole.

Whereas many of Frida's paintings do reflect a self-absorption that was understandable and often justified, this painting suggests an avenue to perfection, harmony and immortality that would never be Frida's within the context of the Western intellectual tradition.

The Judas figure appears again in *THE DREAM* (1940). This time the figure appears to be wired not to entertain as it is destroyed, as in the Western Christian tradition, but to nurture life within the context of the indigenous Mexican cult of death. The scene reflects an image of Frida's actual bed, on the canopy of which lay a skeleton that Rivera jokingly referred to as her lover and Herrera refers to as "an amusing reminder of mortality" [96:142], though Frida needed no reminder of her mortality. Herrera proposes that "he [the skeleton] is awake while Frida sleeps: at any moment, one feels, he could explode, making Frida's dream of death come true" [96:142].

But is it a dream of death that Frida conveys in this painting; or is it a premonition of immortality, even fecundity? In this painting, Frida lies in a dream state, floating somewhere between life and death, earth and heavens. The image of an uprooted vine that encompasses Frida's sleeping figure is no longer that of life emanating from death like the young plant from the earth. Here the dominant image is that of the skeleton-Judas, who, in this painting, is infused with the Ancient American poetic imagery of death, flowers, and immortality. He is wired to explode; but, when he does so, it will be in an explosion of lavender flowers reflecting not death but life and immortality: Frida's immortality.

Using a similar argument, I suggest that *GIRL WITH DEATH MASK* (1938), of which Herrera says: "neither mask seems appropriate for this tiny girl; they accentuate her innocence and hint at the cruelty of her fate" [96:26], may, instead, be viewed as a representation of one small and powerless being, perhaps Frida, perhaps all humanity, standing in defiance of a life, or, better, a worldview, that separates her from the predetermined, harmonious order her indigenous ancestors strove to better understand and incorporate into their societies and rituals.

MOSES (1945), Herrera affirms, reveals Frida's urge to encompass all time and space in "an all-embracing view of the universe as an elaborate web of 'conducting threads'," which Frida referred to as a "harmony of form and color," in which "everything moves according to only one law--life. No one is apart from anyone . . . All is all and one. Anguish and pain, pleasure and death are nothing but a process in order to exist" [95:328]. When, in her diary, she spoke of returning to the *one,* Frida may well have been taking solace in an indigenous-based world view that, in contrast to the ego-centered Western world view, enabled her to subsume her pain and suffering in a nurturing, harmonious whole. Again, in *Moses,* as in her other works, she associates that worldview with the Mexican cult of death and returns to the theme of life, in the form of new green-leafed shoots, emerging from death, represented by two prominently displayed ancient decaying tree trunks.

SELF-PORTRAIT ON THE BORDERLINE BETWEEN MEXICO AND THE UNITED STATES (1932) juxtaposes images of the Western capitalist worldview with those of ancient agrarian Mexico. On the Mexican side of the painting are symbols that clearly reflect key aspects of the Mexican cult of death: belief in the unity of cosmic and terrestrial forces and the Mexican preoccupation with the idea of duality (life-death, past-present, light-dark, and so on).

One of Frida's later works, *THINKING ABOUT DEATH* (1943), perhaps best attests to her growing acceptance of the non-Western Mexican worldview with its cult of death. In this painting, it is death, not Diego, that occupies her mind. Herrrera states that Frida's confrontation with death in this work "is almost Egyptian in its imperturbability" [96:167]. Egyptian? . . .perhaps; indigenous American, assuredly.

Frida Kahlo's life and work reveal a preoccupation with death that is undeniable. But to imply that the theme of death in Frida's work was predominantly ego-centered and Western-based would be to ignore the force of the Mexican psyche in her works. And at the core of the Mexican psyche, both ancient and modern, lies that psycho-cultural phenomenon we call the Mexican cult of death.

We will never know whether the refuge Frida sought in indigenous myth and culture represented a conscious effort on her part to deal with her own unique and painful reality, though there is powerful evidence to support that conclusion. That she consciously utilized her art in the international arena to subtly infuse into the minds of others an understanding of the the roots and richness of Mexican culture is equally probable. Naturally, crucial to that understanding were visions of the Mexican cult of death.

When Andre Breton discovered and became enamoured of Frida's art in 1938, he judged it within the context of the art world he knew, welcoming Frida into the surrealist realm and into the international arena. Though Frida had exhibited her art in the United States, through her husband Diego, the American audience largely failed to appreciate her genius. Subsequent to her "discovery" by Breton, she was invited to debut her work in New York at the surrealist-friendly Julien Levy Gallery. Though reviews of her exhibit were largely favorable, they still did not reflect an understanding of the subliminal, and very Mexican, messages it contained.

Her Paris exhibit in 1939, designed by Breton to introduce not only Frida's art but other elements of Mexican popular art to the French public, was a success, though the gallery had initially rejected all but two of her paintings, judging the others to be too "shocking" for the public [96:167]. Nonetheless, her paintings, all of which were eventually shown, received considerable praise from outstanding surrealists, like Kandinsky, Joan Miró, and Picasso.

Despite a general lack of understanding of the essence of her work on the part of the American and European public, it is likely that Frida accomplished one of her primary goals as an artist, an activist, and a Mexican; that is, she assaulted the international art world with images that, if they did not understand, or even like, initially, introduced into their collective consciousness a vision of the Mexican psyche that even most Mexicans at that time strove to comprehend. And that, for Frida, was revolutionary.

Through her understanding of the Mexican cult of death and the worldview from which it derived, Frida Kahlo may have discovered a unique yet replicable means of utilizing art as a means of insinuating key aspects of indigenous culture and world view into the collective psyche of modern mainstream society. By immersing herself in the dualism of Ancient Mesoamerican culture, she may also have come to view death as a companion, even a gay companion, in her often painful and shortened journey through life.

About the Author

Barbara Brodman is Professor of Latin American & Caribbean Studies at Nova Southeastern University in Fort Lauderdale, Florida. She holds graduate degrees in Hispanic languages and literature, Latin American Studies, and International Business and has published a variety of scholarly works that deal with Latin American and international cultures and affairs. Her 1997 journey through South America, retracing Che Guevara's 1952 motorcycle journey, was widely covered by the media, while thousands followed her adventures online or read her book about the adventure.

Brodman is founder and President of the Global Awareness Institute, an environmental non-profit organization dedicated to preserving and protecting the world's tropical forests through sustainable development. Through GAI, she maintains protected ecological preserves and research centers in the Peruvian Amazon and Belize.

For many years, Brodman sat on the board of the Inter-American Center for Human Rights, and she has served a variety of humanitarian organizations as a trained international election observer and human rights observer. Scholar, humanitarian, and adventurer, Dr. Brodman's knowledge of global and Latin American affairs, and her hands-on approach to acquiring it, enthrall and inspire the many students and non-students to whom she lectures regularly.

References

1. Soustelle, Jacques. *The Daily Life of the Aztecs on the Eve of the Spanish Conquest*. Translated by Patrick O'Brian. New York, 1962.

2. Sahagún, Bernardino de. *Historia general de Ius cosos de Nueva España*. Edited by A. M. Garibay. 4 vols. Mexico, 1969.

3. León-Portilla, Miguel. *Pre-Columbian Literatures of Mexico*. Translated by Grace Lobanov and Miguel León-Portilla. Norman, OK, 1969.

4. Fernández, Justino. *Mexican Art*. Verona, Italy, 1965.

5. Séjourné, Laurette. *Burning Water: Thought and Religion in Ancient Mexico*. New York, 1956.

6. Nicholson, Irene. *Mexican and Central American Mythology*. Verona, Italy, 1967.

7. VanZantwijk, R. A. M. "Aztec Hymns As the Expression of the Mexican Philosophy of Life." *Internationales Archiv für Ethnographie* 48:67-118.

8. Séjourné, Laurette. "Los sacrificios humanos: Religiosos o políticos?" *Cuadernos amerlcanos* 17:127-49.

9. VonHagen, Victor. *The Aztec: Man and Tribe*. New York, 1962.

10. Garibay, Angel María. *Historia de la literatura nahuatl*. 2 vols. Mexico, 1953.

11. Hvidtfeldt, Arild. *Teotl and Ixiptlatli: Some Central Conceptions in Ancient Mexican Religion with a General Introduction on Cult and Myth*. Copenhagen, 1958.

12. Arias-Larreta, Abraham. *Literaturas aborígenes: Azteca, Incaica, Maya-Quiche.* Los Angeles, 1951.

13. Arias-Larreta, Abraham. *Pre-Columbian Literatures.* Los Angeles, 1964.

14. León-Portilla, Miguel. *Aztec Thought and Culture: A Study of the Ancient Nahuatl Mind.* Translated by Jack Emary Davis. Norman, OK, 1963.

15. Ellis, Havelock. *The Soul of Spain.* Cambridge, England, 1931.

16. Velez, Joseph F. "El tema de la muerte en la novela contemporánea mexicana." Ph. D. Dissertation, University of Oklahoma, 1969.

17. Unamuno, Miguel de. *Essays and Soliloquies.* New York, 1925.

18. Ilie, Paul. *Unamuno: An Existential View of Self and Society.* Madison, WI, 1967.

19. Unamuno, Miguel de. *Our Lord Don Quixote: The Life of Don Quixote and Sancho with Related Essays,* translated by Anthony Kerrigan. In *Selected Works of Miguel de Unamuno,* vol. 3, edited by Anthony Kerrigan. Prince-ton, NJ, 1967.

20. del Río. Angel. *Historia de Ia literatura española.* 2 vols. New York, 1963.

21. Castro, Américo. *La realidad histórica de España.* Mexico, 1958.

22. Pritchett, V. S. *The Spanish Temper.* New York, 1954.

23. Ayuso Rivera, Juan. *El concepto de la muerte en Ia poesía romántica española.* Madrid, 1959.

24. Austen, John. *The Story of Don Juan: A Study of the Legend and the Hero.* London, 1939.

25. Huizinga, J. *The Waning of the Middle Ages.* New York, 1924.

26. Ruiz, Juan. *El Libro de buen amor.* Edited by Raymond S. Willis. Princeton, 1972.

27. León-Portilla, Miguel. *Los antiguos mexicanos a través de sus crónicas y cantares.* Mexico,1961.

28. Barnstone, Willis, ed. *Spanish Poetry: From Its Beginnings Through the Nineteenth Century.* New York, 1970.

29. López de Ayala, Pero. *Poesías del Canciller Pero López de Ayala.* 2 vols. New York,1920.

30. Azáceta, José María, ed. *Cancionero de Juan Alfonso de Baena.* 3 vols. Madrid, 1966.

31. Krause, Anna. *Jorge Manrique and the Cult of Death in the Cuatrocientos.* Publications of the University of California at Los Angeles in Languages and Literatures, vol. 1, no. 3. Berkeley, 1937.

32. Azáceta, José María, ed. *Cancionero de Juan Fernández de Ixar.* Madrid, 1956.

33. Salinas, Pedro. *Ensayos de literatura hispánica: Del "Cantar de mío Cid" a García Lorca.* Madrid, 1961.

34. Romanell, Patrick. *Making of the Mexican Mind.* Freeport, NY, 1952.

35. Paz, Octavio. *El laberinto de la soledad.* Mexico, 1965.

36. Nunez, Theron A. "Mexican Attitudes Toward Death." Paper delivered at the Annual Meeting of the American Academy of Psychotherapists, Washington, D. C. , 1964.

37. Ewing, Russell C. , ed. *Six Faces of Mexico.* Tucson, AZ, 1966.

38. Hewes, Gordon W. "Mexicans in Search of the 'Mexican': Notes on Mexican National Character Studies." *American Journal of Economics and Sociology* 13:209-23.

39. Díaz Guerrero, Rogelio. *Estudios de psicología del mexicono.* Mexico, 1961.

40. Gómez Robleda, José. *Psicología del mexicano.* Mexico, 1965.

41. Caso, Alfonso. *El pueblo del sol.* Mexico, 1953.

42. Marks, John. *To the Bullfights Again.* New York, 1967.

43. Tavera A. , Xavier. "El mexicano." *Hispanoamericana* 1:4-18.

44. Jiménez, A. *Picardía mexicana.* Mexico, 1961.

45. Price, W. J. "Birth, Childhood, and Death in Todos Santos." *Practical Anthropology* 13(2):85-99.

46. Garrett, W. E. "South to Mexico City." *National Geographic* 134(2):145-93.

47. Castaneda, Carlos. *A Separate Reality: Further Conversations with Don Juan*. New York, 1971.

48. Castaneda, Carlos. *Journey to Ixtlan: The Lessons of Don Juan*. New York, 1972.

49. Nazoa, Aguiles. *Cuentos contemporáneos hispanoamericanos*. La Paz, Bolivia, 1957.

50. Aguilera-Malta, Demetrio. "Charla con Seymour Menton: El cuento hispanoameri-cano." *Mundo nuevo* 56:49-52.

51. Harss, Luis, and Barbara Dohmann. *Into the Mainstream: Conversations with Latin American Writers*. New York, 1969.

52. Benítez, Antonio. "Prólogo." In *El llano en llamas/Pedro Páramo*. by Juan Rulfo. Havana, 1968.

53. Gómez Gleason, María Teresa. "Juan Rulfo y el mundo de su próxima novella *La cordillera*." *Siempre* 679 (29 June 1966):63-65.

54. Eastman, Richard M. *A Guide to the Novel*. San Francisco, 1965.

55. Rulfo, Juan. *El llano en llamas*, 7th ed. Mexico, 1965.

56. Rodríguez Alcalá, Hugo. *El arte de Juan Rulfo*. Mexico, 1965.

57. Xirau, Ramón. "Juan Rulfo, nuevo escritor de Mexico." *Insula* 16(179):4.

58. Irby, James. *La influencia de William Faulkner en cuatro narradores hispano-americanos*. Mexico, 1956.

59. Estrada, Ricardo. "Los indicios de Pedro Páramo," *Revista de la Universidad de San Marcos* 65:13.

60. Carballo, Emmanuel. *El cuento mexicano en el siglo XX*. Mexico, 1964.

61. Wellek, Rene, and Austin Warren. *Theory of Literature*. New York, 1956.

62. Chávarri, Raúl. "Una novela en la frontera de la vida y la muerte." *Cuadernos hispanoamericonos* 6:174-79.

63. Hill, Diane E. "Integración, desintegración e intensificación en los cuentos de Juan Rulfo." *Revista iberoamericana* 34:331-38.

64. de la Colina, José. "Notas sobre Juan Rulfo." *Siempre* 26:133-38.

65. Couffon, Claude. "EI arte de Juan Rulfo." *Siempre* 714:43-51.

66. Schade, George D. , trans. "Introduction to Juan Rulfo." In *The Burning Plain*, by Juan Rulfo. Austin, TX, 1967.

67. León de Garay, Alfonso. *Una aproximación a la psicología del mexicano*. Mexico, 1958.

68. Torres-Ríoseco, Arturo. *Aspects of Spanish American Literature*. Seattle, WA, 1963.

69. Arenas, Reinaldo. "EI páramo en llamas." *EI mundo*, 7 July 1968, pp. 113-28.

70. Passafari de Gutiérrez, Clara. *Los cambios en la concepción y estructura de la narrativa mexicana desde 1947*. Santa Fe, Argentina, 1968.

71. Revueltas, José. *Dormir en tierra*. Xalapa, Mexico, 1960.

72. Valadés, Edmundo. "EI cuento mexicano reciente." *Armas y letras* 3(4):19-39.

73. Chumacero, Alí. "José Revueltas." *Letras de Mexico* 4:5.

74. Castellanos, Rosario. *Ciudad Real*. Xalapa, Mexico, 1960.

75. Cervera, Juan. "Conversación con Juan Rulfo" and "El gallo ilustrado." *El día*, 16 June 1968, p.3.

76. Donoso Pareja, Miguel. "Algunas consideraciones sobre la joven narrative mexicana." *EI día*, 5 August 1969, p. 12.

77. Reeve, Richard M. "Annotated Bibliography on Carlos Fuentes." *Hispania* 53:597-652.

78. Salazar Mallén, Rubén. "Bombones por el snobismo." *Mañana* 22(11. 119):38.

79. Paz, Octavio. "La máscara y la transparencia." "La cultura en Mexico." *Siempre* 726:iv-v.

80. Fuentes, Carlos. "Chac Mool." In *Seis cuentos Latinoamericonos*. Montevideo, 1969.

81. Carballo, Emmanuel. "Los días enmascarados." *Revista de la Universidod de Mexico* 9. 7:4. 16.

82. Carballo, Emmanuel. Cuentistas mexicanos modernos. 2 vols. Mexico, 1956.

83. Rodríguez Monegal, Emir. "EI mundo mágico de Carlos Fuentes." *Numero* (Montevideo) 1. 2:144-59.

84. Espejo y Díaz, Beatriz. "Carlos Fuentes: Los días enmascarados." *Filosofía yletras* 55-56:261-73.

85. Dueñas, Guadalupe. "Autopresentación." *Abside* 30(3):357-65.

86. Dueñas, Guadalupe. *Tiene la noche un árbol.* Mexico,1958.

87. Congrains Martin, Enrique, ed. *Antología contemporánea del cuento mexicano.* Mexico, 1963.

88. Zepeda, Eraclio. *Benzulul.* Xalapa, Mexico,1959.

89. Azuela, Mariano. *Los de abajo.* Edited by John E. Englekirk and Lawrence B. KiddIe. New York. 1945.

90. Fuentes, Carlos. *The Orange Tree.* New York, 1994.

91. http://www.taipeitimes.com/News/world/archives/2004/05/15/2003155572

92. Frank Bardacke, Leslie Lopcz and the Watsonville, California, Human Rights Committee, trans. , Shadows of *Tender Fury: The Letters and Communiques of Subcomandante Marcos and the Zapatista Army of National Liberation.* New York, 1995.

93. Burns, E. Bradford. *Latin America: A Concise Interpretive History,* 5th ed. New Jersey, 1990.

94. Drucker, Malka. *Frida Kahlo: Torment and Triumph in Her Life and Art.* New York, 1991.

95. Herrera, Hayden. *Frida: A Biography of Frida Kahlo.* New York, 1983.

96. Herrera, Hayden. *Frida Kahlo: The Paintings.* New York, 1991.

97. Paz, Octavio. The Labyrinth of Solitude. New York, 1961.